THE SPIRITUAL JOURNEY

OF A VERY IMPERFECT MAN

PART 1

A ROLLER COASTER LIFE

Graham L Martin

**Kingdom
Publishers**

The Spiritual Journey of a Very Imperfect Man
Part 1
Copyright© Graham L. Martin

All Scripture Quotations have been taken from the New International Version, The
Message Version, New Living Translation and the English Standard Version of the Bible.

ISBN: 978-1-911697-09-1

1st Edition by Kingdom Publishers

Kingdom Publishers
London, UK.

You can purchase copies of this book from any leading bookstore or
email **contact@kingdompublishers.co.uk**

To the lovely Audrie: my wife, sweetheart and best friend

ACKNOWLEDGMENTS

I have been 'best man' at six weddings, and, during my speech at the last one, remarked, "this time I'm determined to get it right". I've no idea how many times the text to this book has been re-written (how could any book at all have been composed without word-processing?), but the fact that it is now probably about as 'right' as I can make it, is down to all the great guys who reviewed it for me.

So my thanks to Kevan Sutton, Rob Glenister, Mike Graveney, John Coe, David Slater, Ian Stackhouse, Paul Ratcliffe, and my old mucker, BC.

Many thanks also to my son, Kevin, daughter, Rachel, son-in-law, Kamran, and my great friend, John Coe. Although you guys may be largely unaware, your contributions during some very 'lively' discussions have given me greater, and much needed, insight into certain topics – cheers!

Most importantly, I really must emphasise how amazing Audrie (Aud) has been throughout all the extreme difficulties of recent years. Without her extraordinary love, commitment and strength, I doubt that I would today be at large in society, let alone capable of writing a book of this nature. She is, and always will be, my one and only soul mate – "friends forever!"

FOREWORD

BY IAN STACKHOUSE

Giving a reason for the hope that we have - otherwise known as apologetics – is an ancient Christian practice and one that has exercised the finest theological minds. Whether it has the power to actually convert anyone to the claims of Christ is an interesting question; I tend towards the view that faith is more existential than it is rational. But even so, apologetics is an important discipline (1 Peter 3:15), and one that demonstrates that faith is not 'a leap in the dark' but a profoundly logical step to take. And I truly believe that this is what Graham has sought to achieve in *The Spiritual Journey of a Very Imperfect Man*. Part 2 is his attempt, and a very good one at that, to reconcile the Christian gospel to the way things are in the world, and to the rigours of human reasoning.

What makes Graham's work fascinating, however, if not unique, is his decision to preface his apologetic with something of a personal testimony in which logic and reason give way to crisis and grace. In other words, even Graham has come to see that for all his questioning (which you become aware of after only a few minutes of meeting Graham), in the end it is love that holds and keeps us – the love of God in Christ Jesus our Lord. Like many people, he has discovered this wonderful truth in the second half of life, so the fact that this testimony is part one of a two-part book maybe is slightly the wrong way round. But either way, I admire Graham for his courage in telling the story and his honesty in opening up on what was an incredibly intense period of his life. It confirms to me something that I alluded to earlier, which is that most people come to faith, or deepen their faith, not as a result of logic but of crisis; although now that Graham has this experience, I suspect his reasoning with people about the Christian faith will simply become even more compelling. It will have that essential warmth and compassion which ought to accompany every communication of the gospel – even apologetics. Whether Graham will possess the same winsomeness when it comes to telling others about his beloved Torquay United, I very much doubt. It is the hope that is the most painful aspect of supporting such a team. But joking aside, I commend this book to you, not out of any sentimental loyalty to Graham, but because I truly believe in theology written from the grass roots.

Rev Dr Ian Stackhouse
Senior Pastor, Guildford Baptist Church (Millmead)
August 2021

PREFACE

This is a book that, from a solely human perspective, could not have been written. In the first place, and most crucially, I should not have been here on the planet to write it. Secondly, certain parts could not have been written without the pain and suffering experienced by me and my family in recent years. Because, if you think (as I did) that things like severe mental health problems can be overcome by simply refusing to feel sorry for yourself and just 'digging in', then you can make very little contribution to a broken world that is often experiencing much hardship and heartache.

The book is presented in two separate but interrelated parts. This first part, which can be read on its own, concentrates almost entirely on my subjective experience, with the second being based on some of the objective evidence, supplemented by relevant background knowledge, gained during my spiritual journey. Amongst other things, the latter explains how the subjective experience relates to a global context and also compares the associated world view to a selection of others, including science.

Every effort has been made to ensure that the book is user-friendly and, hopefully, even humorous (don't hold your breath), possibly helped by the fact that, having been a civil engineer for virtually all my working life, I have never had any religious training as a vicar, priest, theologian or whatever. The intention, therefore, is that the writing should be straightforward and informal, with no associated religious jargon.

This first part covers the lives of the young Graham and Audrie Martin, how we got hitched, the beginnings of our spiritual journeys, and then gradually follows on to how, at sixty years old, I experienced a complete mental breakdown involving multiple attempts to take my own life and a twelve-week spell in a secured psychiatric unit. It is intended that my recollections of this truly horrendous time, and particularly how I survived, will enable anyone presently undergoing anything remotely similar to have genuine hope. Even if your particular tunnel is so dark and so long that you can't imagine, let alone see, the light at the end; don't give up. Sometimes it is ok to not be ok. And nothing lasts forever.

PREFACE

Back in the day, as a young man, I had strong atheistic views and consistently believed the Bible to be a load of rubbish; right up until the time I read it. Subsequent related conversations with any professing 'religious person' concentrated solely on how uptight I could make them, really warming to the task if they started to gabble, rather than on anything they might have to say – a game I called 'Christian baiting'. Audrie, who had a much harder upbringing, was less feisty than me when it came to spiritual matters and did not take part in Christian baiting and the like. Both of us experienced fairly dramatic conversions to Christ in our mid-twenties, although Aud's encounter came out of a place of despair rather than comfort.

Unless referenced otherwise, all biblical citations relate to The New International (NIV) Study Bible: 2000 Edition.

All names, apart from those of close family and friends, have been changed.

CONTENT

PROLOGUE

Monday 5th May 2014, the 24th day in the psychiatric unit, undoubtedly represents the lowest point of my entire life up to now (and hopefully forever!). My depression and, particularly, the stress symptoms were worsening by the minute and by mid-morning, I was pleading with the staff to give me even a small dose of Diazepam or any other benzodiazepine. However, Dr Shah, the resident psychiatrist, was on holiday, and none of the nurses or support-workers was authorised to prescribe drugs like these (they would presumably have been sacked if they did).

The World Championship Snooker final was on the TV, and I had to be rooted to my seat in the depressing communal area to hold off the attempts of various women *inmates* to change the channel. By early afternoon I was almost climbing the walls and felt that I would soon have to start shrieking out uncontrollably (as quite a few did). However, I knew that this would do no good – apart from endeavouring to calm me down, the staff were powerless. I have heard of some heroin addicts, in attempts to withdraw from this drug, actually throwing themselves at barbed-wire fences, hoping that the pain would temporarily distract their minds and give them a few moments respite from the continuous agony – that is exactly how I felt. I was definitely into *having a broken leg in my brain* territory. I could not take any more and simply had to get out of a body that was experiencing such unbelievable torture.

Audrie came over later in the afternoon to pick me up for a *supervised outing*. During the trip, she parked the car in the Waitrose car park, immediately adjacent to Sunningdale railway station and the level crossing straddling the A30.

I was in a desperate state as we entered the store, and felt that I could not face any more; particularly the thought of going back to the unit. Anyhow, as I was looking at the yogurt section in Waitrose, I suddenly realised that this was my opportunity... I was at least 15 yards closer to the open exit than Aud. I must have deliberated for a few seconds, and then suddenly took off, making for the railway and, specifically, the live rails.

I knew I had to get beyond their protective boxing-in adjacent to the station and level crossing, and probably ran about thirty yards up the track to make sure. What I had not anticipated, again completely blinded to everything except the overpowering desire to end my life, was that Audrie would be sprinting up behind me, desperately shrieking in an awful unhuman-like manner for help. There were several people around and although I am sure they were all very concerned, nobody was going to take the risk of also being electrocuted or mowed-down by a train. I got to the exposed electric rail (750 volts, with a high current) and held my right foot over it for perhaps two seconds. These were the most intense two seconds of my entire life! I then placed this foot onto the electric rail, with my left foot remaining on the ground – nothing happened! I tried again, this time running over to and placing my foot on the electric rail serving the other line – identical result. What the heck was going on?

CHAPTER ONE

Introduction to the Very Imperfect Man

I am not and have never been signed up to any social networking sites because (i) I can't be bothered and (ii) I don't think my everyday routine is exciting enough – who wants to know about 'the daily me?' However, if we are talking about what has happened to me during my entire life of sixty seven years or, more importantly, about 24,500 days to date, then, without doing any fancy maths, one would hope that the chances of me writing something interesting are bound to improve. Anyway, here goes. I was born in Redruth Hospital, Cornwall on Sunday 16th August 1953, approximately two months after our present Queen's coronation; so I suppose like the majority of the UK's current population, I am an 'Elizabethan'. I am also one of the *baby boomers*, the generation of people born worldwide between 1946 and 1964, a period of massively increased birth-rates following the end of World War II. In recent times, the most notable events to have occurred on 16th August are probably the death of Elvis Presley (1977) and the setting of the current men's 100 metres world record of 9.58 seconds by Usain Bolt (2009).

My parents Fred and Mary, at forty and thirty three respectively, would have been considered fairly old first-timers for 1950's Britain and had been waiting for a child for almost eight years. The birth was complicated, and my parents were warned that any future pregnancies would carry real health risks to my mother. I was, therefore, an 'only child', a label I have never felt particularly comfortable with (looks like I'm stuck with it now though), and very much loved and spoilt accordingly. This doesn't mean that I was showered with material gifts, most people during the immediate post-war period were fairly poor, but rather that I was given a lot of attention and made to feel I was 'extra-special', whereby my needs and wants were of paramount importance.

My own specialness may have been further reinforced when I passed the old '11-plus' examination, much of the credit for which must go down to enforced additional coaching by my mother, a teacher of English, French and History. My father, a very competent musician (violinist and pianist), had begun his working life as a piano tuner but, with the reduced popularity of this instrument following the war, had ended up as a shoe-salesman; a job he hated. Well, I presume that to have always been the case, because it certainly was by the time I was old enough to be aware of what was going on around me. Indeed, I believe the major legacy he passed on to me was that having a job was to be feared, hated, and avoided if at all possible. It, therefore, never seems to have crossed my mind that one could look forward to and even enjoy jobs and careers - that is unless they were real cushy numbers.

A second much less important, but still irritating, legacy concerned my father's peculiar middle name of *Lennel*; something he had always assumed to be a family tradition going back through many generations of Martins. He therefore also gave me this middle name, discovering some years later that none of our ancestors had it – it was just him and me – brilliant!

I did not make much of an impression upon the county of Cornwall, due mainly to the fact that my parents relocated to Bristol when I was three weeks old. After 18 months in this city, they moved to my father's home town of Paignton, South Devon, before moving again about a year later to Torquay where I grew up. During our time in Paignton, we lived with a married aunt and uncle, Phyllis and Bill, and Phyllis' older sister, Auntie Gwen. All these people were already fairly old (43, 40 and 49 respectively) by the time I entered the world stage. The three of them gave me a lot of love and affection, albeit that Gwen was rather quirky, to say the least. I assume that the reason they all lived together came down to finding the rent money because I don't suppose that Bill was exactly over the moon about sharing a house with his wife's sister, a 'spinster of the parish'.

I never saw or heard of any major rows though. Bill had spent most of the war years serving abroad (mainly India I think), and, in 1942, Phyllis had tragically given birth to still-born twin girls. Again, complications with the birth meant that any future pregnancies would pose significant health risks, and the event was never talked about – people simply didn't. However, on the morning of the day he died some forty years later, Bill told Phyllis that, "Today I will see our girls" – very poignant stuff!

Although the closest family members were all fairly old, the position was even worse for my youngest cousin Alan, again an only child, who lived near Cardiff. His early contacts were my mother's parents who lived in Swansea (nice enough, but came from the generation where *children should be seen but not heard*) and a couple of maiden great-aunts, the Misses Maude and Winifred Crabtree, who resided in Newport, Monmouthshire. These two ladies are worth a special mention. Because there was some ambiguity concerning their county's status at the turn of the 20th-century when they were born, both adamantly insisted that, despite their strong Welsh accents, they were English (they became quite uptight if anyone disagreed with them). Additionally, whatever Maude, the older sister, said was nearly always immediately repeated, more or less word for word, by Winifred. "They've opened a new supermarket in Newport" - "New supermarket in Newport" - you get the picture. This used to crack my teenage mates and me up when *the aunties* were visiting, and we were frequently banished from the house for several hours.

Whatever seemed to be going on in their lives, these great-aunts always appeared to be happy and joyful; something my parents put down to their Plymouth Brethren religious faith. Be that as it may, my cousin John, brought up in Kent with his older brother David (my only remaining original family, Alan having died in 2008), has recently made me aware of a second possible reason. These tea-totalling old spinsters prided themselves on making very good but unbeknown to them, alcoholic, elderflower wine and John reckons that they were sometimes half-cut.

Having passed the 11-plus, I started at Torquay Boys' Grammar School in September 1964. As its name suggests, this was an entirely male school (apart from the secretary), with the various masters usually wearing gowns and, sometimes, mortarboards. All these teachers had nick-names, which usually reflected whether they were popular or not. So three of the better guys were referred to as 'Stan, stand by your beds, Bulmer' (ex-army), 'Tom, Woofles, Majors' (ex-RAF) and 'Don, don't put 'alf a ton in the test tube Martin', Smith (chemistry master, who spoke two languages - English and Devonshire). Those teachers who were less popular had names such as 'Pig', 'Neddy', and, worst of the lot by a country mile, 'Hitler'. This guy certainly looked the part – a fairly short man, with a full head of dark brown hair and a similar styled small moustache. He was vicious, nearly always angry, and not once did I see him smile. Everyone gave him a wide birth, and there was talk that one school leaver arranged for five tons of concrete to be dumped on his front drive. Whether or not this took place is a point of some conjecture, but if anybody deserved it, Hitler certainly did.

Overall, I think I enjoyed my time at senior school. My best mates were Bob 'Gibbo' Gibson and Nick 'Jacklaus' Jackson, both of whom I had known at primary school, and Bill Collins (BC). Although Bill left after only 2 years to go to a Roman Catholic boarding school in Plymouth, we have always remained extremely close friends.

A word of explanation: For a while a whole load of us in our very late teens/early twenties used to go several times a week to Dawlish Warren to play 'Approach Golf'. Even though the course had a maximum hole length of no more than about 150 yards, we all took it extremely seriously, sometimes almost having fights and trying to hit one another over the head with our golf clubs – *only boys having fun*. Anyhow, we all gave ourselves golfing names. Nick Jackson named himself after the great American golfer, Jack Nicklaus, becoming Nick Jacklaus – 'Jacklaus'. I took the name of a lesser-known American golfer called Orville Moody, and for a while was known as 'Orv'. This fairly large group also included Bob Gibson, who could actually play proper golf. It, of course, goes without saying that all the Gibsons who have ever lived are, or have been, known as 'Gibbos'.

I reckon I was a bit below class average when it came to intellectual ability, although probably still fairly good overall, considering that this was the 'A' stream (of three) at a pucker grammar school. In any event, social standing was what counted. I would class myself as 'upper-middle cool', given that, although I never made the long seat at the back of the bus where all the 'super-cools' hung out on away-trips, I did get quite close. This was probably because of my friendship with a very cool guy called Dan Chamberlin, who was great friends with the equally cool Les Richards, who was the best mate of Dave Winters, whose elder cousin, Don, had played football for England and Wolverhampton Wanderers in the 1950s. So pretty impressive!

Actually, unbeknown to Dave, I still owe him a favour. In addition to the dark blue blazers worn by most of the guys, there was an up-market version with red stripes; which my parents, much to my dismay, had insisted on buying. It was only the fact that Dave also wore one of these blazers that saved me from taking a lot of stick and some serious mocking.

Besides all the above super-cools there was a guy called Roger 'Super-Roge' Maplin, who had his own particular brand of cool. Super-Roge is probably best remembered for a stunt he performed on 'Bart', a master with virtually no control over us pupils. I hope this is still fairly funny some fifty five years later. One morning Super-Roge decided to sit the wrong way round on his chair so that he was looking at the nearby back wall. He then put his cap and blazer on the wrong way round so that both faced towards the front of the classroom and fixed a pair of sunglasses onto the back of his head. It's difficult to do justice as to how hysterically funny he looked, and virtually all of us (apart from the *swots*, who were not known for their sense of humour) were just about holding it together. As poor old Bart continually failed to notice Super-Roge at the back of the room, the pressure on us all not to laugh became almost unbearable. So when he finally, after about 35 minutes of a 40-minute lesson, spotted him and shouted out "You there, the boy at the back, what are you doing?" the whole place exploded as everyone became almost paralytic with laughter. And, as far as I know, Super-Roge got away with it completely; thus again, I'm afraid, demonstrating Bart's total lack of discipline.

Time to move on to my present family, starting with how I met my amazing wife. This was on Sunday 5th October 1975 at the Casa Marina night club, Torquay. I was twenty two and Aud was nineteen. I can't remember exactly what chat up lines I used, but by this time I'd developed considerable proficiency in this particular art form;

something not so difficult in Torquay during the summer, due principally to a more or less fortnightly rotation of females on holiday. You always knew that even if the first three women didn't fancy you, the fourth one would. So providing you could take a bit of rejection, your chances of pulling were pretty good.

I guess by the beginning of October I'd have been winding down from the summer season, so may have been a bit more circumspect. Anyway, whatever I said, Audrie went for it and our first date took place on the following Wednesday. This was particularly advantageous, as it enabled me to show off my fantastic car; a 1971, 1.8 litre, brilliant white, Morris Marina – say no more!

As far as I can remember, our relationship seems to have developed and blossomed almost seamlessly from this time. However, Audrie still maintains that, unbelievably, she did not particularly fancy me at first! One of life's many mysteries I suppose. I do know that, in those early weeks, my face seemed to look so fresh and even sparkly, making me think I'd somehow become especially healthy. However, as it turned out, Aud always put glitter over her makeup.

Anyhow, the facts are that we got engaged in December 1976 and were married on Friday 26th August 1977. This was at Paignton Register Office and some of the wedding photos even show people entering the building, which housed several departments, to pay their council rates. There were a couple of reasons for this (why we had a register office wedding, not why people were paying their rates), which are explained in the next chapter. Aud is the second of five children born to Bernard and Beryl – in age order: Steve, Aud, Dawn, Kev and Den.

Our two children, Kevin and Rachel, were born in the Septembers of 1978 and 1981 respectively, and are both brilliant in their different ways. Kev is a very successful and internationally known stuntman, having worked with and doubled for most of the top actors. Rach is simply inspirational, having come through some extremely hard times which would have completely flattened people with less than an iron constitution. She is married to a great guy, Kamran (Kam), and is a brilliant mum to two fantastic children, four-year-old Leon, and eighteen-month-old Jasmine ('Jazy').

No introduction can be complete without mentioning Torquay United FC. What a team, and what a challenge to support them! Something I have been doing now for approximately fifty seven years. Pessimistic people, when you talk to them about how great, say, the weather is, often respond with something like, "Yeah, but we'll pay for it later". That's exactly what it's like when Torquay United put together a series of good results; when is *payback time* coming? Or, to quote John Cleese in the film 'Clockwise', *"It's not the despair, I can cope with the despair; it's the hope!"*

Looking at it from a different angle, I turn to science and, in particular, one of the currently favoured (of numerous) interpretations of quantum mechanics theories and observations. This specific proposal considers there to be an almost infinite number of universes ('a multiverse'), many of which are similar to and *parallel* our own. Accordingly, these particular scientists say, every possible outcome for every possible person in every possible situation is covered; and is indeed currently taking place in one of these universes. Without, at this stage, commenting upon the related science and philosophy, I believe I can boot the whole theory into touch by a single sentence. Can anybody, of sound mind and with hand on heart, actually imagine a universe where it's normal for Torquay United to be in the Premiership and winning on a regular basis!? I rest my case.

CHAPTER TWO

From Atheist to Believer

From about the age of six or seven I was forced to go to church or Sunday School by my parents, or perhaps more accurately by my mother, as I recall her quite frequently being cross with 'Freddie' for falling asleep during the sermons. I can't remember learning anything useful or indeed anything at all (apart from how long this particular form of torture lasted) during these dismal periods, and spent most of the time concentrating on whether anyone could jump from the high roof and live – maybe I also contained stunt man genes.

I can't remember any male adult who attended this church to whom I could look up to or relate, including the minister, the Reverend Gillies. I presume this guy must have had a first name, but I never knew it because my parents insisted on always addressing him as the *Reverend Gillies*.

Different times then, but even from a very young age it seemed to me that my parents simply hovered around him whenever he made a royal visit, making sure he had enough tea (in their very best china cups with almost impossible to hold triangular handles) and cake – "Any more tea vicar?" In my opinion, he seemed to be off another planet, and undoubtedly the sort of person I would avoid if given the choice. In contrast, Jacklaus had a great dad, still alive and living in Paignton at almost ninety five years of age, who used to take us playing table tennis (his family had two cars in the 1960s!), but he, of course, was a *normal* human being and did not go to church.

I managed to get out of going to church by the time I was about fourteen years old; never again (apart from weddings and funerals) to darken its doors, or so I thought. *In the very unlikely event of me ever adopting a religion, it certainly wouldn't be Christianity.* By the time I was fifteen, I had begun the fairly common struggle towards acceptance and establishing my own identity. In my case though, I did feel slightly disadvantaged by being an only child and, much more significantly, by my father, who seemed so unlike any of my friends' dads.

I have already mentioned Jacklaus' dad, but Gibbo's dad, although perhaps less friendly, did at least have a strong and manly persona. My father was and remains the most anxious person I have ever met and, from the age of fifteen, I considered myself to be the *'King Lion'* of the home. I should in fairness point out that he was a very kind man, and that many of his problems arose from significant childhood troubles. I could not, of course, have picked this up in my teenage years, and it was not until I was approaching sixty that I began to appreciate the reasons behind much of his anxiety and also recognise his good qualities – I was thirty years old when my father died, and I did not properly grieve him for another thirty.

My mother was in many ways a remarkable woman. As a teacher, she was the main provider and cornerstone, showing great love and endurance in the way she continued to help and support my father (maybe too much), even though most of the time he was worried about 'everything under the sun'. She also gave me much of my self-esteem, as my incredibly anxious father was unable to provide the affirmation that I suppose all teenage boys need. Almost inevitably his anxiety had led to a nervous breakdown, occurring when I was twelve or thirteen years old, with the apparent *trigger* being the death of my mother's father, Captain E. H. Slater. I simply could not understand why my father appeared to be more affected by this than my mother. However, I can now appreciate that due to his own father's death when he was only thirteen years old, my father probably treated Captain E. H. Slater, who was a very likeable man with a strong character, like a surrogate father. I seem to remember idolising my father up to perhaps the age of twelve but by fifteen, this had changed to virtual contempt. My mother, who had always been very emotional (came from Wales, if that's relevant?) understandably became increasingly so during this trying time. I, therefore, made a firm decision to reject all emotions, or rather the negative ones.

The main way I found in obtaining acceptance from my peers and learning to feel good about myself was through sport, with humour also playing a part. I was reasonably talented at sprinting and football, but later chose first weightlifting and then pole vaulting as I believed that I could obtain greater success in these '*minority* sports'. The related smaller competition pools did indeed create significant advantages up to and including inter-counties level, but not beyond.

I competed for South-West England at junior and senior levels in weightlifting and pole vaulting respectively, and also won the South-West England pole vault championship. However, despite these only modest accomplishments, I remained undaunted as my incredible (but entirely unfounded) optimism still allowed me to dream of successes right up to Olympic level. This meant that I sometimes even practised the award ceremony using a chair when I heard the National Anthem – that life-changing vault was just around the corner! - still is.

For much of my teenage years and well into my twenties sport was, therefore, my '*god*', and I even made a vow, probably at about age twenty, that: "no job and no woman would ever be allowed to get in the way of my sport". This vow finally died the death in the summer of 1994 (then forty-one years old). I was getting ready to bat in a cricket match organised by our good friend Lance Redman when Audrie ordered me to take off my pads immediately and go home to cook a barbeque (hardly the anticipated final lap of honour).

it's quite clear that I wanted to be very different to the perception I had of my parents (particularly, of course, my father) who appeared to be so small and ordinary. So I made it my ambition to aim high, not have a 'pack mentality' and, most importantly, not to be normal – some people reckon I've definitely achieved the latter.

After escaping the nightmare of church attendance, I had decided that all Christians fell into two classes: weird or just plain boring, and therefore set out to aggravate them as much as possible utilising my developing *Christian-baiting* skills. I did not know very much of course, but that didn't matter as long as I got them frustrated or mad, meaning that I had won the argument! Like many of the people I meet today, I seemingly never considered anything they said might represent *truth* or be of any relevance to me.

I used to tell all the various religious folk with whom I came into contact that the Bible had lots of contradictions and errors in it, even though, having read only a tiny fraction, I couldn't name any of them. This attitude of criticising or even condemning a book you've barely read, together with the related inevitable ignorance, is still out there and is quite ridiculous if you think it through. For example, I have attended various combined civil engineering and legal meetings where several of us so-called *experts* have critiqued someone else's report to decide about its accuracy, validity etc. Imagine if when they came round to me, I said, "This report is complete trash, and the person who wrote it is an absolute imbecile who should be locked up. Oh, by the way, I haven't read any of it"

In May of 1974, approaching my 21st birthday, I started a new job at South Hams District Council (SHDC) in Totnes as a drainage technician. 'Being employed' rather than a 'job' is probably a more accurate description of my three years at SHDC, as in the mid-70's this organisation was very similar to a holiday camp, except you had to get up. Many times I used to book out to sites at roughly the same time as Ricky Brown (a really funny guy who had come from a large Vauxhall factory in Luton and felt he'd arrived in 'Paradise') and, following our necessary visits, meet up at various beaches. This carried some risk of course, but we never got caught. You had to be careful not to stay too long in the sun though, because later on, after returning to the office, your face might suddenly glow bright red.

Probably the best time we ever had was during the record-breaking hot and dry summer of 1976 when, one day in early August, we celebrated Ricky's 30th birthday by playing football in our underpants (along with another reprobate called Roger Mills) on Thurlestone Beach, Near Kingsbridge.

Being a drainage technician was very easy and a lot of fun, and it was probably then that I developed my love-affair with the sledge-hammer. Part of the job was to inspect and make notes on the condition of the public sewers, which usually necessitated hitting the heavier manhole covers with the *sledge*. This was because they often needed 'freeing' in order to be levered up, and I achieved the reputation of being the only guy in the whole history of SHDC to have ever broken one of them!

The only job that was easier than being a drainage technician was walking and inspecting the footpaths. This was done by a forty-year-old guy named Ken Payne, whose bad knees meant that sometimes I had to

walk them – what other organisation would let you get away with this!?
One sunny summer afternoon, I had to drive along the beautiful route
from Totnes to Salcombe, check that a gate had a lock on it and then,
after a leisurely pint in a lovely seaside pub, drive back. That
represented the full afternoon's work, and it's amazing that I managed
to ever do a proper job.

The only negative thing at SHDC was that I had a boss, Tom Moffat, who
was religious and, even worse, quite regularly spoke to us about it. This
was really bad news, and I wondered how he had got the job in the first
place given his weird beliefs. Apart from that, Tom was a decent enough
bloke and, to my knowledge, the only one who did any work. His motto
was *work hard and play hard* – me, Ricky Brown and others (including
Ken Payne and another forty-year-old called Dave Lyons, who was
basically a 'smoking chimney') pretty much only did the second part.

One other guy who deserves a mention is Arnold Saunders, later
renamed *Arnie Babe* by the rest of us to try and get him to lighten up.
Arnie was in his late forties and had been in Local Government since
birth. He referred to SHDC as 'The Service' and himself as a 'Local
Government Officer'. He was so institutionalised that he took his coffee
break at precisely the same time every morning, painstakingly opening
his flask using one and a half turns and always carefully eating one of his
sandwiches, which generally had a *sliver* of cheese in them. He was so
predictable that the architectural technicians, who also did very little
work and were located in a parallel hut to ours, precisely mimicked his
coffee break routine behind his back every morning (without him even
noticing!).

Ricky Brown and me had lots of religious conversations and arguments
with Tom, my main aim being to get him to swear; because if he did or,
even better, couldn't answer one of our stupid questions, that of course

conclusively 'proved' that the Christianity thing was a load of garbage. The furthest I got with this was when Tom once told me I was talking absolute rubbish, although the rest of us had also noticed (we watched the poor guy, who remained remarkably patient, like a hawk) that he seemed to be in a bad mood most Monday mornings. We concluded that this was because he'd been with his *nice lovey-dovey* Christian friends on Sunday, and it must have been quite a culture shock seeing a lazy mob like us the following day.

There were a few other *religious types* floating around SHDC, one of whom was called Doug and worked (was employed) in the environmental department. Doug was even more dangerous than Tom - he seemed a good guy, but if you accidentally pressed his 'Christian Play' button he could suddenly launch off at 100 miles an hour into some religious spiel.

I was at SHDC from 1974 to 1977, and during this time there were two particular incidents which had some bearing on my spiritual journey. The first occurred in the autumn of 1974, when, out of the office on a regular site visit, I gave a lift to a hitch-hiker (what's happened to these people - where are they now?). Having done this 'good deed', I did not expect the guy to be so rude and ungrateful by almost immediately launching into a discussion about Jesus Christ and my need to be *saved* (whatever that meant). Anyway, I was seriously hacked off, telling him how sad he was to believe all those superstitious fairy tales and that he needed to get a real life. I think he was probably quite keen to get out of the car after this, and I managed to drop him off after only a few miles. I still accepted, to make sure I'd got rid of him for good, two or three leaflets which I must have stashed away somewhere in my bedroom back home in Torquay.

The second incident, in September 1975, also involved hitch-hiking, this time with me travelling from Gatwick Airport to Torquay following a holiday in Lloret-de-Mar with my mate, Pete Jeffries. Not that great a mate, however, as he subsequently tried to *get off* with Aud when she was already engaged to me. As might be expected, he failed dismally! To increase our chances of getting home at decent times, we split up and I must have had at least five lifts during my homeward journey.

One of the guys who picked me up told me he was not born on this Earth, but came from the *dog-star*, Sirius. Thinking back, however, this claim must surely have related to one of the planets he undoubtedly believed orbit Sirius, as the star itself is much hotter than the sun. Anyhow, he seemed very intelligent and I was impressed with what he had to say. He was also very laid back and simply told me to think carefully about what he had said and make my own mind up.

My next lift was from a vicar – I mean a *proper one*- with a dog collar and other regalia that these types wear. As soon as I told him about the Sirius guy, he warned me to be careful and not to take notice of what was undoubtedly a pack of lies. I think he then, much to my annoyance, sort of preached at me. My conclusion was that this was a very narrow-minded vicar who needed to open his mind up a lot more and basically *lighten up*. It was therefore much cooler for a free-thinking, free spirit such as me to go along with the first guy and reject everything the vicar said.

As we moved into the spring of 1977, I had changed, mainly due to my conversations and arguments with Tom Moffat, from a virtually ignorant angry atheist to a semi-ignorant somewhat softer atheist. I had also begun to ask certain questions, not perhaps directly related to any particular religion or world view, but things like, "Am I my brain?" or, "Is there some sort of 'me' inside my head that is in charge of my brain?" I remember one particular conversation with Tom when he said something like, "If you were to die tonight Graham, where would you go?" I, of course, had no idea. He then closely followed this up by telling me that he had no worries about dying, as he did indeed know where he was going – the outcome, in some mysterious way based entirely on Jesus Christ, was completely certain.

It is hard to now remember exactly what was going through my mind some 40+ years ago, but I had gradually become troubled by what appeared to be something external to me (or could it be part of my imagination?) that was repeatedly trying to communicate with my *inner being* – whatever that was. And this uneasiness increased further when I came to realise the shocking possibility that I might even be asked to give up and hand over control of my life by making some kind of decision - not that any of us have any real control, a point lost on me at about twenty four years of age. I think I had probably arrived at a position whereby I thought Christianity had something to offer, but that it was too narrow-minded for me to adopt. Whoever God was, and I intuitively felt that I was dealing with a being having some form of personality, albeit different to and massively stronger than my own, I believed that any sort of surrender or commitment would mess up my life or at least take the enjoyment from it. I also knew, from the way we all viewed Tom and others with religious beliefs, that a decision to go down the same road would hardly make me popular, and I wanted people to like rather than reject me – simply *going with the flow* thus seemed the much easier and safer bet.

My approach had always been to *live and let live* or *if it feels good, do it*, and I certainly did not want to become some kind of religious freak or narrow-minded fanatic. My parents' and grandparents' generations seemed to be all about doing something in a particular way (including religion) because it had always been done that way and *settling down*. I wanted to avoid all that sort of stuff like the plague. My 'gospel' for life, if you could call it that, was to stick by your mates, to stay clear of work by achieving fame and fortune through sport (I'm still waiting for that), and to enjoy yourself to the maximum, immediately getting rid of anything that caused unhappiness, because, as we all know, *you only live once* and *you're a long time dead*.

The only Christian who had ever impressed me at all was Tom Moffat, and what if he'd got it wrong? – what a waste of a life! Some sort of battle was going on within me and it was growing more intense.

I employed delaying tactics, as I desperately searched for some kind of middle route. I certainly knew I was no saint, but then again, perhaps not too bad either. So that if there was such a thing as Heaven, then I reckoned (or perhaps hoped) that my good points and deeds would sufficiently outweigh the bad ones and I'd get in. However, what the overall pass mark might be, was anybody's guess.[1]

Anyhow, things continued to happen, the first being that Jacklaus became a Christian. This was quite a shock, as he was such a laid-back guy and, in line with my thinking at the time, surely not the sort of person who would require religion or anything else to prop him up. I was not, of course, going to take the mick out of him and so listened to most of what he had to say. He was going to a Pentecostal church in Brixham, and Audrie and I went a couple of times to check it out. It was livelier and, on the whole, better than what I'd had to endure growing up, although people repeatedly shouted out, *Praise the Lord* and *Preach it*

---

[1] Although this thought process would have been foreign to me at the time, is the principle of judgment based on good versus bad points or deeds even valid? I mean, if I'm in court for a driving offence (as has happened), it surely wouldn't help my case if I told the magistrate that I was always kind to animals and old ladies.

Brother, which tended to jar on us a bit. They also kept praising Jesus Christ for forgiving them their sins by dying on the cross. After a while, I felt like saying "yeah, you've said that a lot of times now – get over it!" However, all in all, it was an ok experience and we did learn some stuff. Nevertheless, we both felt that going along a couple of times was enough and did not feel any need to go back.

A few weeks later I was training at a farm on the outskirts of Torquay. This was where, in the previous autumn of 1976, I had rented a field for £20 a year and constructed a pole vault landing area plus run-up for about £120, instead of buying all the stuff new at about £4,000 – who says I can't do DIY!? This got me, in the November, on to BBC's local TV programme, *Spotlight South-West,* with the well-known interviewer, Roy Lipscombe (who!?). Audrie came to watch me vault and be interviewed, along with my good friend, Brian 'Bozo' Brockington, who wore his new bright yellow, cord trousers especially for the occasion.

In between vaults (now back in the spring of 1977), I found myself thinking about life, which was simply awesome at that time. I was getting married to a very beautiful woman and we were going around Southern Europe for a month via train and camping, and honeymooning for three weeks in Barbados. My pole vaulting was also going great. I thought, *Graham mate, this is probably about as good and as easy as life gets*; and, from a solely human viewpoint, this seems to have been borne out by subsequent events. Yet, I also remember thinking at the time: *Is that it? – it's all very wonderful, but is there anything about life that I'm missing out on?*

Amazingly those leaflets, grudgingly accepted from the religious hitch-hiker in 1974, somehow turned up. All I can remember was a single sentence from the New Testament (NT), *I tell you, now is the time of*

God's favour; now is the day of salvation [2]. (2 Corinthians 6:2b) I don't know exactly what I understood from this, but I unquestionably experienced an *upping* of the pressure to make some sort of decision.

I have already described how difficult it is to remember precisely how I was feeling at this time, but I think it was a bit like being pursued by an extremely intelligent, perhaps even all- knowing, being who I didn't seem able to shake off and dismiss from my mind. And yet this being was not that frightening or even particularly intimidating (a perception of my mindset at the time, rather than necessarily good theology). Anyhow, in the end, I made a sort of prayer to whomever I felt was talking to me which, I guess, was essentially a demand or challenge. It went something like: "Ok God, if you're real and you're there, please convert Bill Collins (BC)". At that time, Bill had been in California for almost a year and we hadn't had much recent contact. The last time I'd spoken to him about anything religious, we concluded that all that stuff was for weak people who needed some sort of crutch and certainly not for cool characters like us. (easier to take this view when you're young)

BC's Roman Catholic boarding school education from the age of thirteen onwards, although it probably instilled some good life skills, gave little indication of a similar resultant positive effect for matters religious (at least from my perspective). He was, from his mid-teens onwards, a real 'ladies man' and I learnt much of this craft by directly observing him. We had been to Roman Catholic mass on Christmas Eve a couple of times in our latish teens, both drunk as skunks, and it certainly took all my resilience not to crack up laughing as the priests in their long *dresses* went about all the various mumbo jumbo and superstition. BC was also a very clever bloke (definitely still is) and a pretty decent middle and long-

---

[2] The word 'salvation' in this book is always taken to mean rescue or deliverance from harm, ruin, or loss.

distance runner (definitely still isn't). However, despite all these skills, I think he could have achieved even more if he had realised his talents more fully and, perhaps, been a bit more committed – e.g. he got a third-class honours degree in law from University College, London when a first or certainly an upper second would have been within his compass.

Anyhow, coming back to my prayer to God or whomever. The next day (possibly the day after, but certainly no later), I was gob-smacked to receive a long letter from BC in California saying within it, "for the first time in my life I'm 100% committed to something or rather someone, and that someone is Jesus Christ!" What I did not realise then, or indeed for many years following, was that this letter dated back four months, Bill for some reason having waited before posting it.

I phoned Bill up the same evening (on or about April 28th 1977), and told him where I was at spiritually and, particularly, how freaked out I was by my prayer being answered. He was really surprised that I was open or even interested to hear what he had to say, because he'd assumed that, once he told me what he had done, I'd think he had become some sort of religious *nut*. Once Bill realised this was not the case, he encouraged me to take a step of faith by inviting Jesus Christ into my life. Now that did sound a bit nuts, as I was still against anything religious or churchy, so much so that I refused to even sing hymns at wedding services.

Nevertheless, after a considerable time of wrestling with so many of my thoughts, both for and against, which of course also resulted in significant extra expense to my parents' phone bill, I did eventually say those words. They did not feel like a formula or anything, but rather a conscious letting down of my defences so that they meant something like, "I don't really know who you are, but if you're the God who made me, and are therefore able to do a whole lot better with my life than me, then take it – I'm handing control over to you".

The day following my phone-call conversion, I was back at SHDC talking to Arnie-babe, when I suddenly said, "You know, Jesus has helped me a lot Arnold".

He said "eh" and I thought, *eh, what's going on?*

"Yes he has". I said.

Arnie was very surprised because previously he had only heard me use the name of Jesus as blasphemy. (for Christ's sake, etc. – still so prevalent today)

Tom Moffat was hovering around and said something like, "Praise the Lord", which, although very friendly, made me feel rather uncomfortable. I also suddenly found that I wasn't swearing or blaspheming, which meant that I had to start using other adjectives to compensate. This wasn't easy, as I had not realised that swearing and blasphemy formed so much of my everyday speech. Nevertheless, after a while, I did manage to become a fluent English speaker without using expletives.

Tom suggested that I try reading the Bible, and particularly the New Testament. I wasn't sure about this because, possibly due to attending church as a boy, I had on several occasions in my early twenties tried to read the Christmas story during this festive period, presumably out of some form of loyalty or respect. But I could not read it for long – it was too boring. However, within a few days of my conversion, an amazing thing happened. I again could not read the Bible for long, but this time because I was getting too excited. The words were leaping out of the pages of the New Testament and hitting me – I had to keep going out for runs simply to cool down.

This experience represented evidence of being *born again*, something that Jesus explained to Nicodemus, a Jewish religious leader (see John

3). However, in 1977 and being in Torquay (hardly the cutting edge of society!), I had never heard of it. It was like a fire burning up inside of me; well described by two, previously downhearted, followers of Christ who met Him on the road to Emmaus shortly after His resurrection. As soon as Jesus left them they said, *"Were not our hearts burning within us while he talked with us on the road...*(Luke 24:32) I was also filled with very great joy. I think that happiness comes primarily from our life circumstances, whereas joy comes from God and supersedes these events, good or bad.

I appreciate that my circumstances were very good at the time, but I had never experienced joy like this before - it was incredible - bring it on! I, of course, had no problems with positive emotions, whereas anything negative, such as potential crying or weeping, would automatically have been swallowed up by denial. My negative emotions thus remained frozen, a situation that continued for approximately the next thirty five years.

Sadly, as it turned out many years later, I did not think that there was much wrong with me at the time of my conversion, and so any repentance[3] would probably have been no more than nominal. I simply did not want to miss out on something which could be to my benefit. The consequence of this was that my conversion, although undoubtedly real and exciting, resulted in more or less everything and nothing being changed.

---

[3] Repentance is essentially genuine sorrow for past wrongful behaviour and a deliberate decision to radically change course. In other words, a 180-degree turn – if you're driving along the M40 hoping to get to Birmingham and you see signs for London, you need to repent. The writer, C.S. Lewis also points out that our repentance is, at best, fairly limited and that only a perfect human being would be able to repent perfectly; and they wouldn't need to – clever sod. Anyhow God, thankfully, takes us on from where we are at the time of our conversion.

Everything because I realised that my atheistic approach to life did not hold water intellectually (so congratulations to me - I did at least back down on something), and nothing, because not much of my newly found knowledge seems to have been transferred from my brain to my heart or soul - sometimes called *The longest journey in the world*. Indeed, although there continued to be some notable exceptions, my overall Christian journey gradually became more cerebral and pride-oriented. This is a particularly relevant quote from Tim Keller, a New York pastor, *"Believers understand many doctrinal truths in the mind, but those truths seldom make the journey down into the heart except through disappointment, failure, and loss."*[4]- yep, that's a fair cop.

This is how it was for me. I started going to church and, amazingly, enjoyed it - it was suddenly relevant. Actually, for many years I couldn't quite get over the fact that I went to church; sometimes I would be sitting there thinking, *what am I doing here?- I'm an atheist*, only I wasn't! Tom Moffat thought it was great, and said that I would never regret what I had done; something which has now, over forty years later, been proved to be wholly true. Tom also told me I was making incredible progress, and, I suppose, from a solely intellectual viewpoint, that might well have been the case.

I had so many questions[5] and was always talking about the Gospel - down the pub, in nightclubs or to anyone who would listen. I did not talk about it quite so much at SHDC however, because once the news of my Christian conversion got out, most people were unhappy about it. So now they *took the mick* out of me and Tom. As I had pretty much

---

[4] Tim Keller, *Walking With God Through Pain & Suffering*. Hodder & Stoughton, 2015, p.5.

[5] I reckon one of my reasons for asking so many questions related to what I considered to be the shallow answers given to me by certain Christians or religious types before my conversion (stuff like, "We believe it because it's in the Bible"); and I did not want to be like that, it made my blood boil.

expected this outcome, it did not particularly surprise me; and it is notable that Jesus said to his disciples, *If people listen to me, they will also listen to you and if they persecute me, they will also persecute you.* (John 15:20) I was hardly getting persecuted, but I'd certainly crossed over some invisible line; meaning that, amongst other things, I was no longer 'one of the boys' - get this - Jesus Christ is not and has never been, neutral.

I suppose all this begs the question, *What did Audrie think about all this?* This is explained in some detail in the next chapter, but she was, amongst other things, fairly bewildered. During the planning of our wedding about six months before, I had said something like, *"There's no way it's going to be in a church, as I am not making promises to a god I don't believe in and probably doesn't exist anyway";* now here I was completely changing tack only a few months before tying the knot.

Although the consistency of this attitude does, of course, make sense, I think that quite a bit of my strong opinion related to the fact that I did not want the hassle of a formal wedding and preferred to spend the money on the three-week honeymoon in Barbados – which was fantastic.

I almost went mad in the lead-up to Christmas 1977. What were people doing? Christmas wasn't about buying loads of presents, getting drunk, going to parties and all the other stuff - It was about Jesus Christ. I obviously had a very short memory recall, because I'd spent all the Christmases since I was about 16 doing precisely those things.

In early January 1978, we moved to Peckham, South-East London, where I did mini-cab and taxi driving for about six weeks (call sign 'Victor 7') before starting an honours degree course in civil engineering at The City University, London. Tom Moffat had given me the name of a local church

(The Spinney), and I went along on one Sunday evening about a week after moving to Peckham.

I don't think I have ever felt so out of place in my life! It was like something from the 1850s. The preacher, The Reverend Dai Harris, had a short *back and sides,* old-fashioned greased back hair-cut, and was immaculately dressed in a black suit with matching black tie. He carried a huge black Bible under his arm as he meticulously mounted the wooden steps into an old pulpit and solemnly addressed the congregation. I ought to say, as I look back now, that he was undoubtedly a *man of God* but I could not, of course, see this at the time.

The fairly small congregation were also very formally dressed as if they too came from the mid -19th-century, and I desperately looked around for someone who might remotely have something to do with the 1970's. I eventually saw this guy (Steve Fawcett) who appeared more modern and *normal* than the rest and decided to seek him out when proceedings finally ended. However, by that time, I was so depressed that I more or less bolted out of the church managing to avoid speaking to anyone.

What of course I did not know was that Steve had also seen me, and God had said to him, "That young man will be your life-long friend." Steve told me later that this particular experience had not happened to him before and never with such clarity since. He was therefore very confused to find out that I had left before he'd had a chance to talk to me. Anyway, I suppose I had walked briskly about 200 yards when I just knew I had to turn round and go back inside the church. So I did; met Steve, and we've now been best buddies for over forty years.

CHAPTER THREE

From Agnostic to Believer (Audrie's Story)

Audrie's and my upbringing could hardly have been more different. As the second of five children, her life was pretty tough and also involved a major role in bringing up her youngest brother, Den, eight years her junior. Although so very young herself, Aud's influence during his early years seems to have been very positive; he has turned out to be a great guy.

It appears that the general tone of Aud's life dates back to those early times. She's so often been willing to take a back seat and help others live their lives and achieve their dreams. Aud spent most of the first ten years of her life in the then-Lancashire town of Warrington, moving to Torquay at the beginning of 1967.

The spiritual atmosphere in her family home was predominantly atheistic, and she cannot remember any Christian books being around. That is apart from a big family Bible, with a picture of Jesus Christ (no doubt *westernised*, but so what) forming one of its pages. Audrie says that, as a young child, she often felt drawn to this picture and even loved Jesus through it. There is a song called, *There's Power in the Name of Jesus* and, certainly, this is a strong indication of God's hand on her life from a very young age. Her gran and some of her aunts and uncles also appear to have held Christian beliefs, and Aud thinks that it was their influence that resulted in her being christened as a baby.

When I first met Aud, spiritual issues of any sort were irrelevant to our relationship. I remember getting very angry at my previous girl-friend, Elaine, with whom I went out for almost three years, when she said she believed in God. I think I told her she was talking absolute bunk (that's the polite version) and needed to sort herself out. I would quite like to see her again now to put the record straight, although I very much doubt that this will ever happen.

For the first few months of my relationship with Aud, I was still seeing Elaine from time to time. In fairness, Aud was also going out with other blokes on the quiet. I don't think there was ever much doubt that Audrie and I would end up together, but BC was a bit concerned that I might not make the right choice. One day he said to me something like, "What you've got to consider, Orv (we were still in that era), is how each one is going to deteriorate as they grow older; I tell you, Aud is going to show much less wear and tear than Elaine when they get old, say into their thirties." - wise words mate.

Life in Peckham was hard, particularly after the very cushy three years at SHDC. I was also ill-prepared for university, thinking that, as I had already obtained a higher national certificate (HNC) in civil engineering, I would be able to *walk* the degree course. This misplaced confidence lasted about twenty minutes of the first lecture, aptly named, *stress analysis*. Things even grew so bad that in May or June, I dropped out. I suppose this was hardly surprising, given that my main reasons for taking this degree were to train at Crystal Palace where there were indoor pole vault facilities, and to justify to my family why I was giving up a *job for life* at SHDC to take six months off to travel and do other things. Audrie had simply wanted to start a new life away from Torquay. Anyhow, I did somehow manage to get back on the course after about two weeks, and perversely was helped by the fact that one of the brighter guys, called Jonathan, had suddenly packed it all in; apparently due to Ipswich beating his beloved Arsenal in the 1978 FA Cup Final.

What happened was that I suddenly realised I was not, after all, the worst student at The City University, and, hey, I was still there! So there you go, more positive thought patterns were beginning to develop. Audrie did brilliantly, holding down a succession of secretarial jobs so that we were eligible for a 100% Greater London Council (GLC) mortgage and thus able to buy 61A Naylor Road, Peckham - a one bedroom ground-floor flat, with reasonable sized rear garden – for the princely sum of £7,250. The cost of this mortgage varied between £50 and £60 per month, which was less than half the going rate for renting a similar property. I know the word, *God-send,* can be overused, but certainly not in this case. Without this flat and its garden (which was ideal when Kev came along), I doubt that we would have been able to make a go of it in London.

As often happens following the birth of a first baby (in Torbay Hospital), Aud's hormones had gone a bit haywire by the time she returned to Peckham with Kev at the beginning of October 1978. As a twenty two-year-old new mum, she became very depressed; which was hardly surprising given that, due to lectures, laboratory classes and study, she rarely saw her still-new husband, we had very little money, and she had no friends or social life.

She had, of course, met Steve Fawcett and his wife, Jo, but was very wary of them, as she believed that the three of us were plotting to get her to their church. She did come once, however, and hated the experience. She felt that I pushed her too hard to go down the *Christian Road*, and I guess I probably did. I became increasingly frustrated and impatient, because I knew that an encounter with Jesus Christ would turn her whole life around - and she'd be happy again. I think I even said to her at one time, when she was very angry and depressed, that our marriage depended upon her becoming a Christian – you won't find that in any book on Christian evangelism or counseling. Nevertheless, whatever my shortcomings, I did at least continue to regularly pray for her.

We kept going with a pretty strained marriage and, if it had been a realistic option, I reckon Audrie might well have taken Kev and gone to live with her parents in Torquay; at least temporarily. By early Spring 1980, I was still struggling hard at University, Audrie was generally very unhappy and depressed, and our marriage was just about hanging together. In reality, and I can certainly see this now, she did unbelievably well to stick it out in London for three years, two of them looking after a baby with virtually no help[6] and only in her early twenties.

One of the *clubs*, if you could call it that, at The City University was the Christian Union (CU). I did not particularly like it though; it seemed a bit too formal and stilted for my taste so I rarely went along. However, in March 1980 the CU organised an outreach event to get the Christian message across to as many students as possible. On the bill were Roger Forster, the leader of the Ichthus Fellowship in Forest Hill, S.E. London and Steve Flashman, a musician from Guildford. I had been hoping to take along a couple of my University mates, Kevin Marshall from Yorkshire and John 'bluey' Davison from Brisbane. However, they cried off at the last moment and so I went on my own.

The event was surprisingly good, and I ended up talking to Roger Forster at the finish. I was still struggling along at The Spinney, attending only because of my great friendship with Steve Fawcett. Roger said it would do me good to come to Ichthus, which certainly belonged in the 1980s. When he found out I was living in Peckham, he introduced me to someone from Camberwell who said he would give me a lift the following Sunday. This guy, Graham Warner, became a great friend for many years, although we have now lost contact.

---

[6] There was very little children's TV and, apparently, no play-zones in those days.

Graham duly picked me up on the Sunday, and Audrie also came along. It was the weekend the clocks went forward, and spring was in the air. Ichthus was incredible and so laid back, particularly when compared with the atmosphere at The Spinney. It was predominantly young, with a high percentage of students, and undoubtedly relevant to the 1980s. There were, however, older people as well, and I specifically remember a lady in her nineties, Rose, (I think) praying passionately to God. Her prayers were so personal, so intimate – it was obvious that she knew Jesus very well. I am sure that the form of worship, particularly the very lively music, would have been foreign to this old lady, who probably grew up singing slow and ponderous hymns from centuries past - but it did not matter, she was there to praise the God she loved and just went for it big-time.

Roger Forster preached, in his usual very laid-back style, which I thought was fantastic. Aud, however, was not so impressed, seemingly having no particular interest in what Roger had to say. She did, nevertheless, say that Ichthus was much better than The Spinney – most of the women at least wore make-up. She also liked Graham and related well to his wife, Sallie, who read women's magazines and was pregnant.

I went to Ichthus from Spring 1980 onwards and was disappointed that Audrie had not found anything inspirational enough for her to come again. I, of course, assumed that this was route-one to her becoming a Christian, as it would surely only be a matter of time if she was regularly exposed to Ichthus and Roger's (or any of the other leaders, including Graham's) preaching.

By early August 1980, I had completed my finals and obtained an honours degree in civil engineering. However, we still had virtually no money (I had no job and was signing on), and our marriage was distinctly rocky. I remember sitting alone on the bed one afternoon bemoaning our circumstances when I know that God spoke into my mind saying something like, "Cool it, it's all under control."

I have noticed two specific characteristics of God's style when giving *Words* – firstly, He is very concise; using the minimum number of words necessary and secondly, there sometimes seems to be subtle and gentle amusement concerning something so big to me, yet so small to Him. We had got to know Graham and Sallie reasonably well by this time, and one day Graham said, "You need a holiday – I'll fill my car up with petrol and you can have it for as long as you want". This was a pretty amazing offer, particularly as it had only been three to four months since we'd first met. We all went to Torquay for two weeks. Not surprisingly, this act of kindness impressed Aud, and her new relaxed friendship with Sallie built upon her relationship with Jo, who had been a faithful friend for over two years. Audrie and Jo used to go to, amongst other things, pottery classes with the lovely Roland!

HOW GOD SPEAKS

This is a subject that may well be unfamiliar to some people, and it is therefore hoped that this brief explanation will be helpful. There have clearly been, and indeed still continue to be, instances where people have actually heard or hear an audible voice. However, it seems these occasions are definitely in the minority, and that it is much more common for God to communicate via the (apparently) intuition parts of our spirits. Christians refer to these messages as 'Words of knowledge and/or wisdom', both of which are mentioned in the New Testament. For the purpose of this book, the abbreviated form, Word or Words will always be adopted. In addition, it needs to be admitted that sometimes believers can get these things wrong; so great care is necessary, particularly if we feel that God is telling us that a certain person is going to be healed from some ailment.

Forward to Sunday 7th September 1980: Aud and me were having a very bad day and arguing a lot. In the early afternoon, the arguments reached their crescendo with Audrie threatening to burn all my Christian books. I then had the weird experience of almost losing my temper, but at the same time praying like mad. I knew that our relationship was in real trouble. I remember shouting at her something like, "OK, but you tell me which books and precisely why you want to burn them."

We then split up. I think she went into the front room and I took Kev for a bath. I did not often do this but, for some reason, decided I also needed a bath (possibly to allow me to calm down). We were in the bath for only a few minutes I think when Aud came in. She'd been crying and was very upset. She said, "Will you come and pray with me?"

I don't know exactly what happened to Kev, but he must have got out of the bath at some stage. So there I was, standing in the front room holding a towel and dripping everywhere. I then prayed for Aud who knelt on the floor, praying passionately as she surrendered her life to Jesus Christ, asking for him to come in and take control. To be honest, it all felt really amazing and almost unreal.

Everything calmed down after this, and the next day Aud brought me a cup of tea in bed; this was a very good sign as she hadn't done that for ages. When she opened her mouth, she simply could not stop talking about how amazing she felt - so full of joy and unbelievable happiness. It was almost too much. Graham and Sallie, even though they had seen many dramatic conversions before, seemed slightly taken aback over the awesome and immediate changes in Audrie. She had been extremely depressed for about two years, and then suddenly, she wasn't – just smiling and beaming all the time. I obviously knew what was happening and had, of course, predicted (I know it was in an utterly inept way, but it was still accurate!) that an encounter with Christ would turn her life around.

This seems to be how God often likes to work. I'd told Him, in no uncertain terms, that He needed to get Audrie to Ichthus so she could listen to a top preacher, whereas He'd decided to do the job without any of that; dragging me out of the bath would do just fine. It's God's gospel and he knows best.

However, the magnitude of this whole event had taken even me by surprise. Not only had Aud been very depressed for two years, she had also often taken the mickey out of me for being a *goody-two-shoes* or something less polite. Now she wasn't even sure that I was a proper Christian (in one way, maybe I wasn't, but that's another story). I know this sounds ridiculous, but the changes in her were so great that I was even looking behind chairs and under tables in our flat to see where God was! She then announced that she wanted to get baptised in the swimming pool at Ichthus House on the Wednesday evening of the following week– that is only ten days after her conversion. The 1st-century church baptised new converts within a day or even a few hours, but in our times it often follows attending some sort of weekly course – we certainly know how to make simple things complicated.

Sometimes called *Believers Baptism*, because it is a public witness to something that has already happened privately, this voluntary act makes perfect sense. The immersion under water represents identification with Christ in His death and burial, and the rising up from the water represents identification with Christ in His resurrection and new life. However, all of this was almost becoming too much for me as it seemed one minute Aud was too depressed to go shopping (although she always did, bless her), and then the next minute she wanted to get baptised and speak to maybe one hundred and fifty people.

On the actual Wednesday, I was *sweaty armpits* all day. I could hardly believe how someone so very depressed for so long might suddenly be ready to speak in public to so many people. But Aud had the transforming power of God inside, and it all went extremely well and, actually, fairly easily. She was baptised on the evening of Wednesday 17th September 1980 by Graham Warner and a guy called John Sims.

I would not normally include the *Baptism Verses* given to Audrie, which were written in a special card and are of course personal to her. The reason I do so is that they were rather mystifying at the time, being unlike the usually positive messages given on these occasions. Instead, these verses, from an Old Testament (OT) prophet called Isaiah, said:

Fear not, for I have redeemed you; I have summoned you by name; you are mine.   When you pass through the waters, I will be with you; and when you pass through the rivers, they will not sweep over you. When you walk through the fire, you will not be burned; the flames will not set you ablaze. For I am the Lord Your God... Your Saviour. (Isaiah 43:1b-3a)

I believe everyone has seen definite proof of this in recent years, without taking anything away from Aud who has been truly amazing.

One final point: it is important to emphasise that not all conversions to Christ are dramatic or even consciously known about at the time. A reasonable analogy might be that when you cross into Devon from Somerset using the A303, you immediately go past a signpost which says *'Welcome to Devon'*. So you instantaneously know you have changed county. However, if you are walking cross country (across Exmoor), you don't know the precise moment of changing counties. But in both cases, you've definitely *crossed over*.

CHAPTER FOUR

Adrenalin Man (15 - 57 years old)

This is a quotation from *The Compassionate Mind* by Paul Gilbert, a renowned secular psychologist,

> *Some people think that the best way to get through life is to be insensitive to one's own pain, to block it out and just get on with the job, develop a hard skin. To be compassionate is to be respectful of this process of trying to become 'hard-nosed' or 'thick-skinned', to acknowledge that we're all trying to get through life the best way we can. For some people, however, these tactics can lead to mental health problems or a certain callousness that could spell trouble for others. Training our minds to be more in tune with ourselves - our upsets, feelings and needs - is usually more helpful to us.*[7]

This quote accurately describes the way I lived much of my life from about fifteen to fifty seven years old and is also consistent with my complete mental breakdown at the age of sixty. Of course, as a postmodern psychologist in early 21st-century Western society, Gilbert can't definitively say that my tactics for getting through life during these forty two years were wrong; but they undoubtedly were on certain occasions, particularly, I believe, from my early fifties onwards.

---

[7] Paul Gilbert, *The Compassionate Mind*. Constable & Robinson Ltd, 2013, p.221.

The related episodes included the death of my mother in January 2005, when I was fifty one. Although I did arrange a few crying slots as I knew this would be good for me (so incredibly controlled!), there was no way I would reveal any internal upset during the time up to and including her funeral at which I spoke without any emotion. I simply thought this was being incredibly strong and, perhaps unbelievably, *Christ-like*.

So why did I behave like this? Resulting in my life being *maxed out* by the time I was approaching sixty – as Gilbert warns about and so accurately describes. Firstly, it is now clear to me that so much of my life was based, largely unconsciously, on a determination to be completely different to the perception I had of my father. He was so anxious and weak during the period I knew him, that my endeavour to be exactly the opposite is probably not so surprising. Indeed, some people make very serious life mistakes by simply not wanting to be like a particular parent, or as an overreaction against specific childhood memories, rather than on the facts that lie before them. Polarisation is accordingly a fairly common trait at both individual and corporate levels.

Secondly, probably due partly to genes and partly to an *only-child syndrome* whereby I frequently felt the need to prove myself, I have always been very competitive and often prepared to go to extremes. Running more or less in tandem with this has been the fact that I was blessed with a high energy constitution. Thus, although my preference, particularly concerning work, has always been to have as easy a time as possible, difficult circumstances have often dictated a change to the default approach of keeping going full-on, not looking right or left, and continually pouring in more effort and adrenaline until job-done. When called upon, this technique, as noted below, seems to have been reasonably successful for several decades - that is it often got results, but, as per Paul Gilbert, *watch out for callousness.*

The attempted denial of all negative emotions from about the age of fifteen clearly had a major effect on the development of my thought patterns and associated opinions. But, preventing worry, fear and similar emotions is not normally possible in our anxious and uncertain world, particularly in the proximity of an ever-fearful father. So I ended up bypassing this particular problem by using denial and avoidance, as per modern-day psychology parlance, to exude what appeared to be a relatively untroubled persona. I accordingly developed an integrated hard outer protective skin, effectively my *external unreal me,* which attempted to conceal all my internal flaws and weaknesses. This skin formed the main part of my survival strategy for years, and probably even decades, by keeping difficult and potentially worrying problems at arm's length. I believe this type of behaviour is not particularly uncommon, but serious problems can arise when someone's *external unreal me* becomes significantly removed from their *internal real* me (in totality, or limited to certain areas) - that is fooling ourselves is the worst and most dangerous delusion of all.

This approach strengthened my disdain towards my father, and, by becoming increasingly estranged from him, I guess I must have inevitably rejected some reasonably healthy parts of my own being. I think *the apple never falls far from the tree* covers it, but I would not have had any idea of this at the time.

As I progressed through my teens, as the *king lion* of the home, it became apparent that I was simply too strong for my parents to challenge some of my incorrect and, probably, often shallow opinions. These presumably concerned making sense of the world, or rather what was most relevant to me in the 1960s and 70s South Devon. I, therefore, gradually morphed into, at least in my own eyes, an increasingly important person, who had to always be heard (loudest voice) and have the final word on most issues. I certainly could have done with more boundaries and limits that would have hopefully curbed my egocentricity and provided a more realistic view of my actual identity and related limitations during this phase of maturation.

Although we surely need to know who we are, all of us also need to be equally aware of who we are not. However, with hindsight, my father was obviously in a very bad place, and my mother was probably worn out from looking after the two of us and holding down her full-time job as a teacher. I now understand that this was not a particularly healthy situation for me to be in, albeit much better than those who have experienced only cruelty rather than love when growing up.

The following quote is from Richard Rohr, a Roman Catholic priest and writer, who, in his helpful book, *Falling Upward*, confirms and clarifies the nature of the shortcomings relating to my upbringing. He says, *...without law in some form, and also without butting up against that law, we cannot move forward easily and naturally. The rebellions of two-year-olds and teenagers are in our hardwiring, and we have to have something hard and half good to rebel against. We need a worthy opponent against which we test our mettle....When we are only victorious over small things, it leaves us feeling small.*[8]

I think there is little doubt that my father largely failed me in this area when I was in my teens, and perhaps even into my twenties, whereas I believe I was a worthy opponent at that time of Kev's life. He was incredibly powerful; full-on *fast bowling* compared to the late *spin* developed by his clever little sister as she grew up. As is fairly common for fathers and their *sweet little daughters*, there were very rarely confrontations, especially in the early years, between Rachel and me.

---

[8] Richard Rohr, *Falling Upward*. John Wiley &Sons, Inc., 2012, pp.25-26.

It's clear in my mind that my father, who certainly exhibited the attribute of gentleness, was a better father to me in the early years than I was to Kev. This was predominantly due to continued anxiety on my part that he might turn out to be similar to his weak grandfather. I was, therefore, unduly hard on him during the period of his life from, say, six to twelve years old. Mistakes like this almost always come home to roost, and our relationship accordingly suffered.

Indeed the main resulting problems were only finally resolved some four to five years ago when Kev confronted me about those early years of my parenthood. One of his great qualities is that he will usually commence difficult discussions by saying something very positive; in this case, complimenting me on the high energy and *never say die* approach that he reckons I have passed onto him, and ultimately enabled many of his stunting achievements. But then, "in other areas, dad, you've really screwed me up."

Unsurprisingly there followed a fairly lengthy and rather emotional discussion, which ended with me asking for and receiving his forgiveness for those early years. Without his positive reaction, I believe we would both have had trouble moving on. For most of us, parenting is not at all easy. There is a famous poem called, *This Be The Verse*[9] by the poet Philip Larkin which is particularly relevant in this respect.[9] Although its content is probably not appropriate here, It can easily be found on the internet.

Even though the above problems were not ultimately sorted out until many years later, Kev and I gradually became a lot closer from his mid-to-late teens onwards, with sport unsurprisingly contributing greatly to our relationship. I even took on quite a bit of his sprint and stamina

[9] Philip Larkin, This Be *The Verse* – 'High Windows' collection, Faber and Faber Limited, 1974.

training during the time he was a youth team player with several football league clubs. As I was still competing in athletics myself, it was a pretty good match up. We did have our moments though. For instance, towards the end of our training together (in August 1995), we were about to start our normal Frimley to Deepcut (and back) run of a little over three miles, and, as is not particularly unusual for a forty two-year-old dad with his seventeen-year-old son (two alpha males), we were not in best moods with each other.

In actual fact, considering that this run contained a fairly long hill, our times of around twenty one minutes were pretty decent. Anyway, as we finished limbering up, Kev asked me for the car keys and when I asked, "What for?" he replied, "So I can listen to the radio while I wait for you to finish". Red rag to a bull or what!? There was absolutely no way I was going to agree to that so, as we set off I was determined to win or at least finish a very close second. Anyhow, even though I thought I might get him on the last hill rise, he did, to his credit, hold on to win by seven seconds. At the finish, as we were both stretched out over the car bonnet trying desperately to get some oxygen, I did manage to gasp out, "So why aren't you listening to the radio?"

The following illustration appears to be particularly relevant to my spiritual life. I remember, back in the autumn of 1978, sitting in a certain maths lecture at The City University. Maths is like everything else (including, of course, sport) - you can be good at a certain level, but not when taken significantly beyond this. As I sat there, it was obvious that I was outside my comfort zone, and not only me - others too were also struggling. The problem was that the guy giving the lecture was a brilliant mathematician. These types are usually the worst lecturers because they've probably never encountered some of the difficulties that are affecting the rest of us *plebs* - they've always seen it all as very obvious and cannot understand why people are moaning.

Anyway, the lecturer spent maybe twenty minutes covering the blackboard (we were still in that era) with masses of Greek symbols, and a few numbers thrown in to make us feel a little more comfortable. He must have done this about three times, wiping off the blackboard in between and allowing us to breathe. Then at the end, he turned around and asked, "Any questions?" One big and particularly loud guy at the front shouted back, "Yeah, how do you do it?"

Up until comparatively recently, I'd only intermittently given serious consideration to making that question a real priority concerning Christian living; frequently giving more attention to the answering of peoples' questions than to my spiritual journey.

It must, of course, be emphasised that there is nothing wrong with having questions; they are important in avoiding the situation of someone simply being carried along on a wave of emotion with very little factual knowledge. My problem has been that the factual stuff has often outweighed experiential knowledge, thus hindering close relationship and worship.

Despite the difficult circumstances from January 1978 onwards, I still managed to hold on to and presumably even added extra layers to my hard outer protective skin; something that, in addition to its principal survival role, had caused me to become increasingly insensitive to other peoples' needs and problems. If you think things like severe mental health issues can be overcome by simply refusing to feel sorry for yourself and just *digging in*, then you can make very little contribution to a broken world that is often experiencing much pain and suffering.

As it happens, it seems that this *skin,* albeit unconsciously built to ensure that I would not turn out to be like my father, was both a success and a failure. The thing is, my father appears to have been stressed out about virtually everything, but particularly socialising and work where he was petrified. He came home in a terrible state, sweating and shaking, virtually every day. Nevertheless, probably due to some positive genes in conjunction with a very loving upbringing, the sociability part of my hard outer protective skin appears to have been fairly true to the *internal real me* – so not too many associated problems.

However, I had some real difficulties on the work front. Not surprisingly, I'd been so affected by my father's extreme anxiety in this regard that the only way I could deal with a *proper* job (not of course at SHDC, where being able to socialise was the main prerequisite) was to use extreme energy and denial to get through. The three years I spent working for Cyril Parker, 'Parky', between 1980 and 1983 (twenty seven to thirty), are a prime example of this. Although a brilliant mathematician and theoretical engineer, Parky was gauche (socially inept) and simply could not relate to me at all. I think he must have grown up playing with his *Meccano*® set and had probably wanted to be an engineer from an early age, whereas my aspirations, which were mainly sport-related, could not have been more different.

The result was a one-to-one relationship between a brilliant but gauche, middle-aged man and a mediocre and internally freaked-out young graduate engineer. I did not even want to be there, and often woke up gagging at the thought of going to work. Nevertheless, despite my work anxiety inheritance, I believe I could have handled Parky much better if I'd had any real passion for my job and maybe brought in a bit of competitive edge – something like, *stuff you - I'll show you what I can do!* But I did not. My hard outer protective skin was being stretched and distorted, but somehow again, it did not break.

It seems clear that any weakness built into your character at an early age, in my case the belief that having a job was to be feared, hated and avoided if at all possible, can become very much reinforced and heightened by any related experiences in adult life. I think, deep down,

Parky was a decent enough chap, but that this was generally hidden by his lack of even average social skills. Anyway, he bullied me mentally, on one occasion pointing out a short-term student with the practice and saying, "Look at him, he's going to be a really good engineer; but you won't, you haven't got what it takes." (not that you need to be *Brain of Britain* to succeed as a civil engineer!)

I include this illustration to show how Parky's gaucheness could max-out. He was extremely long-winded and used to write very long reports and letters. One day he was dictating a letter to a loss adjuster called Mr Clark. So he starts off the letter, "Dear Mr Clark", and then goes on and on until finally, "Yours sincerely, C. Parker". Then, and get this, "ps. I understand that since dictating this letter, Mr Clark has now died". That was it, nothing more!

At the end of the three years, I left Parky to start my own business and a Master's Degree course in Geotechnical Engineering ('Geotechnics') at the University of Surrey in Guildford. Geotechnical Engineering includes foundations, retaining walls, basements, slope stability analyses, ground investigations and related subjects – so pretty sexy stuff. One of the main reasons for this was that I was still looking for a method of avoiding hard work, this time by hopefully ending up as a lecturer with long holiday periods. Unfortunately this did not work out as lecturing posts had, by then, become much more demanding than before.

Although I enjoyed the above course overall, I had to again employ my default approach as previously defined, which was for me to get through life as an *indestructible* person (yeah, right!). This can actually work when you are young, but becomes a real burden as you get older. The Swiss psychiatrist, Carl Jung, had something to say on this and I quote him in part 2.

I must also say, in fairness, that Parky did teach me a few vital things which enabled my business to enjoy both success and longevity. One of these was how to avoid calculation errors, or at least spot them before anyone else. I reckon I probably got the great majority of mistakes out of my system just by working for him, and it's clear that he did not have the best of me either. Finally, the problems arising from all these blunders resulted in the addition of *selective perfectionism* (not including DIY) to my default approach to life.

A particular irony is that, despite Parky being a better mathematician and theoretical engineer than I was, the advent of computer technology meant that I eventually undertook more prestigious and difficult jobs than he ever did. My business (1983 – 2013) also lasted ten years longer than his, so there!

Within five years of starting the business, I had obtained my MSc in Geotechnical Engineering and also passed the very demanding examinations for chartered engineer status. I put these successes down to three factors: God massively blessing me, tremendous support from Aud, and working like a lunatic (rather different than at SHDC). In fact, for the chartered engineer exams, I was regularly putting in about fourteen hours of study per day - nowadays; I find it hard to even be awake for that long. So I guess this is a specific instance of my default approach paying dividends.

I again owe Audrie *big-time* for my chartered status as I nearly went to the wrong exam venue; a total cock-up that would presumably have resulted in instant failure. The night before the examination she found an official letter advising that due to ongoing refurbishment works at the 'hallowed' institution building, this usual location had been changed to a nearby hotel.

Another example of when my default approach not only paid dividends but probably represented the only feasible way forward concerns a truly horrendous event that took place in the summer of 1990. Even now, some thirty years later, it would not be appropriate for it to be identified and described; suffice it to say that it rocked and essentially shattered both the larger family and our own small unit of two adults and children aged eleven and eight years old. Nothing prepares you, as a husband and father, for correctly handling circumstances like these. Anyway, in the aftermath, and for the next few years, I really *dug in* and held the family together. This period probably represents the high point of my life to date.

This next episode and, in particular, its eventual legacy probably also added a further layer or two to my hard outer protective skin. It concerns a sermon given by a guy called Ray Miles, in the early 1990's. Ray, who is a lovely guy, was preaching at Ichthus and Audrie's brother, Den, had gone up with me to South London as something of a one-off. The theme of the message was: *If you're a Christian, don't ever say that you're just or only human.* The point here is that the Christian life should be Christ-empowered, meaning that we have the potential (hopefully resulting in actuality) to live beyond our natural resources. His power, rather than our willpower, should thus make the vital difference to us overcoming and conquering the many problems that life offers up.

However, *Adrenalin Man* eventually got this teaching completely upside-down concerning two very major incidents that took place in the summers of 2005 and 2006. The first one occurred when Rach went to Thailand on her own, and then one Friday morning, after she'd been there for about two months, phoned to say that she was very ill and believed she was going to die in that country - so we would never see her again. She also thanked us for being good parents. Audrie took the full brunt of the message, and I have to say that she was amazingly calm by the time she phoned me with this news. I was on site in North London and was not at my best because, contrary to the client's assurance, I had just received a £50 parking fine. All I can remember is leaving the site and walking aimlessly along the pavement outside feeling a mixture of numbness and complete panic.

Then, after about ten minutes, this *Word* (and I don't get many) powered itself into my brain, *It's not what she says* (about dying) *that counts, but what I say*. This massively calmed me down, and I even continued to work that afternoon. Aud and I got lots of people to pray, and Rach accordingly landed at Heathrow Airport on the following Monday afternoon clearly very unwell, but alive! Although it took a considerable time, she did eventually make a full recovery.

The second incident occurred in August 2006. I was working like a total maniac with bigger and bigger, and more and more important jobs. One afternoon I began to feel very ill and simply had to go to bed. As time went on, I felt worse and worse, and hotter and hotter with a temperature of 40ºC or 104ºF. My hands began to sweat and shake uncontrollably. I was eventually taken by ambulance to Frimley Park Hospital, feeling so bad that I believed I was experiencing a fairly major heart attack. Indeed, I thought I was going to die, and even felt a bit excited about the prospect. When I did not die, this turned to slight disappointment. Not that I wanted to leave all my family and friends at this time, it was more that the presence of Christ was almost tangible.

So what was wrong with all this? Nothing, to start with. The results of both experiences had been very positive, and I was very grateful to God. I knew that it was only His involvement that had prevented two major tragedies from devastating our family. However, it would appear that, as the years went on, I very gradually began to take the credit myself for both these very positive outcomes and, particularly, how I had reacted.

On both occasions I had managed to tick the right boxes on the *How to be a Successful Christian* questionnaire and, most importantly, had also ticked a further box of *How to let others know*. In other words, I was nurturing a *spirit* of pride and hypocrisy, characteristics that God appears to hate most of all.

This seems a good point to take stock of the overall development of my business and how it affected me as a person, both psychologically and spiritually. In the early years, when work was often scarce, God taught both Audrie and me that we could rely totally on Him. The Lord's prayer, still fairly well known in this country, has the line within it, *"Give us each day our daily bread (Luke 11:3)* but for quite some time we were living hour by hour – work simply came in at these intervals as it was needed, and with a large mortgage and young kids, it certainly was. This led to increased trust and gratefulness, and I accordingly thought of the Lord as my main client. I even enjoyed the work for most of the 1990s, primarily due to the fact that it was fairly straightforward; mainly house subsidence, and thus not to be feared. However, these jobs reduced dramatically towards the end of the decade as insurance companies began to deal with the majority of subsidence problems in-house.

I consequently needed to reinvent myself as a consultant civil engineer (geotechnical and, in part, structural), and rapidly became computer-literate as I began to take on much larger construction projects with, not surprisingly, very driven clients and tight deadlines. The majority of my projects related to London and the South-East of England, generally considered to be the most driven and aggressive when it comes to the work-place within the UK.

By the start of the new millennium, I was feeling very stressed and pressurised, again using denial to keep much of this at bay. Nevertheless, although not in a good place overall, I still managed to step up to the plate by plugging into my default approach and utilising the old favourites of adrenaline and more effort.

In any event, as life went on, the business became more and more successful. It was like a *bleep test* – the older I grew, then the harder I had to work. So I became more manic as the business became my *god*. I did not appreciate this though, as I never thought of myself as any type of workaholic. This was because the very negative work ethic engendered in me from an early age meant that, apart from intermittent exceptions, I struggled along and did not enjoy what I was doing. As I did not enjoy work, I thought I couldn't possibly be a workaholic – a bit like eating loads of chocolate but thinking that as long as you weren't loving it, you wouldn't put on any weight. You'd think I would have sussed this out, but there you go.

The much larger, multi-million-pound construction schemes that had replaced house subsidence problems were extremely demanding, involving very complicated reports and calculations of maybe 200 pages in length.

The following outline examples represent three of the more complex projects:

- Calculating the potential movements and increased stresses relating to Victorian brickwork tunnels encompassing main railway lines a short distance from King's Cross/St. Pancras Stations, due to the proposed construction of a five-storey building directly above with 7m clearance between the building foundation and the tunnel crowns.

I did the extremely complicated calculations (iterative – going round and round for evermore - Christmas 2000 was a lot of fun!) using 'Excel', with some much-needed help from my good friend and fellow geotechnical engineer, Daniel Masters (he was a real *God-send*).

Anyhow, I think at some stage, the client, Alan Kingston and Associates, had doubts that I was getting all this right and called in a very high-brow consultancy (GFC) as a check. The people who make up this firm are, and have generally always been, professors or cutting edge researchers, with state of the art (often self-written) software. Unbelievably, they came up with basically the same answers – God knows how (well I presume he does). Kingston's were very impressed and gave me quite a lot of work after this.

- Designing an approximately 6m deep basement in 2010 using secant piling, the closest sub-structural wall of which was only some 3m from a railway line serving the nearby Shepherd's Bush mainline station.

This project made it onto the Grand Designs TV programme, and several people I've talked to remember it because the basement, which functions as a dance area (an absolute *must* for any home), has a gaudy psychedelic floor.

I was watching the associated programme some twelve months after design completion and saw a stonking great goods train ambling along the section of track adjacent to the closest basement wall. By this time I had, unsurprisingly, largely forgotten the finer points of my design and could not remember if I had allowed for the surcharge loading arising from this type of train or for the much lighter multiple units. Anyway, I shouted at the TV screen for the goods train to keep going. I did think at the time that, if I had not designed for the heavier case, it would have been picked up by Network Rail's overseeing engineers but, even so, mistakes can still get through. However, after about an hour's panic checking, I discovered that I had indeed designed for the maximum rail loading possible – so all OK. I have also not heard of any problems during the nine or so years since the basement construction; the client (Maycox Piling Solutions Ltd) presumably being satisfied with my input. As I guess it is for most jobs, the *praise* I normally received was just an absence of *aggro*.

- Interpreting the findings of a 2010 ground investigation so that design could be undertaken for massive concrete pad foundations relating to the largest construction project for Scotland that year.

The chief problem was that my client, Ed Pulford of Newfield Site Investigations Ltd, was a *Yeah Yeah, no problems mate* type of guy, and had given the main contractor a completely unrealistic date for my interpretative report. Indeed, this date came and went even before I received the necessary factual data (borehole logs plus lab testing results). When this data did eventually arrive, I was under great pressure to produce the report *immediately*.

Only Ed knew that I was working from an office in my own house, and even he did not know that, once the report had been dictated, I was waiting for my typist, Colleen, to come back from her keep-fit class. So there is a situation here whereby this very large and extremely expensive construction project in Scotland completely stalls while waiting for a guy in a converted back bedroom in Surrey, who in turn is waiting for his typist to return from her Water-Workout session. I think I made light of it at the time and even passed it off as a humorous incident; however, I now believe this to have been pure denial and that I was significantly affected by the huge amount of pressure.

On top of this, there were the intense periodic stresses due to my geotechnical legal work as an expert witness for various clients, including Network Rail.

Looking back, I occasionally shudder about the magnitude and importance of many of the jobs that I took on. In reality, the total amount of work involved was both stupendous and stupid. I presume that being able to cope with this related partly to still having a high energy constitution and, more importantly, to long-term sustainment by God throughout all the many and various associated problems.

Aud, Kev, Rach and BC warned me for several years, especially after my illness in the summer of 2006 (Pneumonia), that my life was heading towards some sort of calamity, but I wasn't listening. I was too much *into* myself and would not step back to calmly assess the current situation. I was also fearful that if I stopped or eased up on the business, I would not get going again. I suppose I was becoming robotic. Moreover, the increasing stress also began affecting other areas of my life, but not by so much.

When Brendan Foster was once asked what he considered to be the athlete, Paula Radcliffe's, best quality, he replied, "She doesn't listen to other people, but simply does her own thing". When he was also asked about her worst quality, he again replied, "She doesn't listen to other people, but simply does her own thing". This is about the best spin I can come up with concerning how I had become.

As described previously, my default maxim of keeping going full-on, not looking right or left, and continually pouring in more effort and adrenaline until the job is done had resulted in certain successes; some of the more extreme circumstances perhaps even meriting this approach. Anyway, I simply assumed, probably unconsciously, that I would always be able to do what I'd always been able to do. So, against all advice, I pressed on with the business in like manner by continually bullying myself, including insisting on *perfection* for every job. I also fooled myself that everything was OK because I had, in the end, become very successful. During this time I was earning a lot of money and had obtained the nickname of *The Guru*, both of which I liked and, almost certainly, gave me much of my identity. Not that I understood this at the time, thinking that, as a Christian, my identity was grounded in Christ; this may have been the case once, but no longer.

Obsession with keeping my business on track and bullying myself accordingly, in time resulted in me also bullying Audrie; not physically of course and, to the best of my knowledge, never putting her down in public. However, you can do a lot of damage to someone by repeatedly disrespecting and refusing to take any notice of them. After all, Audrie was an equal partner and administrator in the business. She was (and is) a beautiful woman, looks much younger than her actual age, and has a great personality. I'm sure that those people who had some idea of what was going on must have thought I was completely off my head to act in this way.

So why did I bully Aud and essentially make her the scapegoat for all my (denied) stress? Primarily because she was there. It is surely not healthy to be in the proximity of your wife when business pressures are going ballistic, although I would still prefer this to a commute up to London every day.

I managed to convince myself that being flat out, although very unpleasant, had certain merit to it; perhaps not so difficult in a culture that makes a virtue of busyness and exalts self-made men and women. So if I needed to stay up to 3am to get a report out, I simply did it – more effort and more adrenalin. And when I did not see a similar attitude reflected in my wife, even though she was very supportive, I became frustrated and aggravated. I continued, of course, to demand perfection from myself on the work front, and wanted to see evidence of this in

Audrie. Not surprisingly, she was considerably turned off by all of this, and our relationship consequently became more and more strained.

Any imposed rivalry with your marriage partner, whatever the cause, greatly diminishes the relationship and you both end up missing out on so much. And, without doubt, loss of respect causes love to die. Attempts to change others are always doomed to failure; only God can do that sort of stuff, and so the best we can do is to respond positively to His endeavours to change us. And, surprising to most of us, letting Him do this will result in the flourishing of our humanity rather than being to its detriment. In any event, as is now abundantly clear, *by this time I had strayed far from the Christian walk; the path was still there, as reliable as ever, but I was falling off it.*

Negativity or disapproval consistently aimed at your marriage partner soon becomes a habit, so you get used to criticising them more and more. In time you cannot, or perhaps refuse to, see the damage you are doing to the person you love the most. And with hindsight, it seems that, although I had denied and buried all negative emotions (particularly work-related), this only resulted in them being buried alive. And they had been tunneling upwards for a long time before they eventually broke the surface, causing the *madness and mayhem* described in the following chapters.

As 2011 commenced, I was still under a very high degree of work pressure and, having been *maxed-out* for over ten years and taken on jobs which were at the extreme upper end of feasibility for a *one-man-band*, I was inevitably now tiring. Not that I admitted this to myself; I was in too much denial. I might have perhaps felt a little less pressure if, having paid off the house mortgage in 2008, we hadn't borrowed some more money to purchase a property in South Wales which was then rented out. The profitability of the firm over the previous four years had been fantastic. However, it seems that I was generally much more client-driven than money-driven so, on balance, the result may well have been more or less the same. In some ways, my life was similar to the M25 motorway; as long as absolutely nothing goes wrong the traffic flows fine, but even the smallest of problems can cause a total standstill.

As a final illustration of what was happening to me, I cite my participations, during the early 1990s, in the Great South Run at Southsea, without noticing hardly any of the various and quite interesting landmarks that I passed during the races. I was simply focused on getting *good* times. Now, I do not believe there is much wrong with this attitude, as long as it doesn't result in looking down on those who take a more relaxed approach which, incidentally, I probably did. It's a ten-mile race, for goodness sake. If you want to run hard, then run hard. If you do not want to have any awareness of what is going on around you then, so what? It's only fifty minutes out of your life (*I wish*). But what is the result when this blinkered approach encompasses all, or virtually all, of your life? – *madness and mayhem*, as above.

Back in the mid-1990s, Aud and me had gone to a meeting at Bracknell, where the speaker was a Welsh guy called Rob Parsons from Care for the Family. Rob, an ex-lawyer, is an excellent orator and I can still remember some of what he said in a talk titled, *Anything can happen to anyone*. Although I guess this is a bit pedantic, it would surely have been more accurate to use the title, Anything *bad* can happen to anyone.

I have to be realistic here and say that any chance of me being picked for the England football team has probably now gone. Playing for Torquay United is of course still a strong possibility, particularly now I'm in my sixties. Anyway, on the afternoon of Sunday 13th February 2011, a chain of events that I would never have believed possible was set into motion.

CHAPTER FIVE

An Ever Downwards Trajectory

I had never experienced back problems before and was, therefore, not particularly alarmed by a slight to moderate pain in the lower part of my spine during the three to four days leading up to and including the morning of Sunday 13th February 2011. I concluded that this pain was due to the hand-augering of boreholes (if you don't know what this is – you haven't lived) and a couple of training runs earlier in the week (probably correct), and that it was, accordingly, nothing to worry about (definitely incorrect!). I thus ignored it and went for a two-to-three mile afternoon run on the Basingstoke Canal footpath.

Later that same evening, my back became extremely painful. Neither our doctor, Dr Lyndhurst, nor the NHS physiotherapists, nor my osteopath, Damien, diagnosed a back issue; and indeed Damien said it was a sacroiliac joint problem and gave it a really thorough going over to hopefully improve matters. In the end, it was a blind Guildford physiotherapist, Rupert Griffiths, who correctly diagnosed a herniated disc and, within the next week or so, an MRI scan (which we paid for - couldn't wait for the NHS) showed that a fragment of disc had sequestered (broken off) and was pushing directly on the nearest nerve. It seems probable, because any back injury should be treated very delicately, that the sequestering of the disc had been caused by Damien – but whatever, all water under the bridge now.

The pain was unbelievably bad, and I have read somewhere that nerve-related problems of this nature are the closest a man can get to the horrendous pain experienced during childbirth. It was certainly far more painful than the worst imaginable toothache (also nerve-related) and completely unrelenting, making it necessary for me to get up through the night to have the hottest baths bearable every two hours or so, simply to feel some momentary relief. Unsurprisingly, it was also virtually impossible to stand for more than about ten seconds, and once, when Audrie temporarily mislaid the car keys, I had to lie on the bonnet until she found them. Dr Lyndhurst prescribed Tramadol® (gives good pain relief, but morphine-based and often results in nasty side effects), and I took the maximum dose of this drug together with the maximum dose of Panadol® (paracetemol) for four to five months.

My constant use of this overall medication, combined with sitting in a certain position at my desk, enabled me to lose only eleven working days. One of my clients at the time even offered to double my fees if I could get up and continue with his project during this brief non-working period, but it simply was not possible. A friend's wife, when employed as a doctor for the NHS, took six months off for what sounds to have been a very similar injury. In April we paid for private consultations and an epidural injection, which at least reduced the raw pain from a category *nine* or *ten* (agony) to about a *six*.

If I thought I was working hard before my back problem, the pressure now ramped up big-time. On the evening before BC's wedding in June (It was my sixth time as a *best-man*), I was designing an extremely urgent and difficult underpinning job and, following its completion at about 10.30pm, experienced almost no sleep due to withdrawing from Tramadol - one of the side-effects of this particular drug. I was furthermore still in considerable back pain, and beginning to feel nauseous.

I firmly believe that my extensive use of Tramadol, the side effects of which include suicidal tendencies, most probably started my addiction to prescription drugs – it certainly triggered a slippery slide.

As time went on, my back pain began to reduce further and I became reasonably comfortable but the nausea was getting worse. Sometimes the associated symptoms were so bad that I could hardly sleep, and, for several months before starting work, I had to take approximately one-hour early-morning walks belching all the time. This may sound funny, but it wasn't. Indeed, on two occasions, I drove instead to the A&E department of Frimley Park Hospital at about 6.30 am and, following fairly extensive blood tests, was prescribed the anti-emetic drugs, Metoclopramide and Cyclizine. After lots of delays and hospital appointments, gall bladder problems were eventually diagnosed near the end of November.

Work was becoming so difficult due to feeling nauseous most of the time, but I still kept going and managed to meet all the usual tight deadlines. At this stage, there was only a slight drop-off in output. However, I was, not surprisingly, getting near the end of my tether, and so we again decided to *go private* to avoid joining the fairly long NHS waiting list for gall-bladder operations.

This example illustrates just how arduous work had become. One day in December 2011, when again feeling very nauseous, I was under great pressure to produce a construction drawing for a site in West London by the close of play. I was also getting to grips with a new computer, which did not help matters. Anyhow, I psyched myself up to simply push through in consecutive fifteen-minute segments and did not leave my chair for six hours; twenty four lots of *fifteen-minutes* with no coffee or toilet breaks. The finished drawing was finally emailed to the piling contractor client at the end of this period. The head of the firm was accordingly very thankful, but it was becoming increasingly evident that to keep working like this, was unsustainable.

The gall bladder operation took place towards the end of January 2012, and for the following couple of days, I felt pretty good with only minor nausea symptoms. I, therefore, thought I had survived and *saved* the business, which had been my main concern. I did not even think about Audrie and my family - total and utter loss of perspective by this time. Anyhow, the next day the nausea was back and I felt even worse than before the operation. Now I had absolutely nothing left and experienced a partial mental breakdown.

One Sunday afternoon a couple of weeks later, I was feeling so bad that I attended the out-patients at Frimley Park Hospital. The on-duty doctor realised that my nausea was at least partly due to stress, and prescribed a fairly short-term course of Diazepam*, an anxiety-relieving drug of the Benzodiazepine family. This resulted in immediate improvement, and I even got back to working forty hours per week. Although this was still about twenty hours less than my normal working pattern before the operation, it still represented an immense improvement, and, I guess, was eminently more sensible.

However, the fact that Diazepam is an addictive drug and should not be continually taken for more than about three weeks escaped the attention of a succession of young doctors who had replaced the long-serving Dr Lyndhurst after his retirement in September 2011. I, therefore, stayed on Diazepam for month after month (from my viewpoint, it was keeping me in business - the most important thing – right?). A second anxiety-relieving drug, Fluoxetine*, was even added. Both of these medications carry warnings relating to the possible triggering of suicidal tendencies.

In July 2012, I was prayed for by Leif Hetland, a Norwegian evangelist who has witnessed God do amazing things, such as healing the deaf and the blind, at various places around the world. Leif did not shout or touch me, but held his hand about a foot away from my head and spoke very firmly and authoritatively. I simply could not stand up and collapsed to the floor. I then experienced what felt like *fingers* working within my stomach. I felt really good when lying on the floor. It is hard to describe but I was in a sort of semi-conscious and very relaxed state. This lasted, I suppose, for about twenty minutes.

However, soon after getting up from the floor, fear returned big-time. I knew I had been touched by the power of God, and then I panicked, thinking: *I won't have a better chance than this to get well, so what if even this doesn't work?* And, *When am I going to come into contact with someone like Leif Hetland again?* Actually, this reaction does have some validity. Although it is undoubtedly God rather than any human being who ultimately provides the healing, He has given Leif a very special, and probably not that common type of ministry. So what had actually happened to me?

My best explanation is that the nausea was being caused by two separate factors. The first was that some six months after my gall bladder operation, my digestive system was still not working properly, and, without doubt, God healed that. I know this because I was very soon able to come off my restricted diet and eat virtually anything. Secondly, experiencing nausea over such a long period had developed into a phobia whereby even the normal stresses of the day, compounded of course by business pressures, resulted in both the continuation of this symptom and in related clinical depression. Both of these were then exacerbated by guilt resulting from not being able to fully trust God following Leif's ministry. I became even more stressed and depressed as time went on.

Aud has also experienced the above phenomenon of *going out in the Spirit*, which is one of the reasons it has been included. She is simply not the type to invent or exaggerate anything and up to that point, had been very sceptical of this particular occurrence. She was standing next to me in another meeting when a healing evangelist began to speak Words of knowledge – that is telling her things about her life that he could not possibly know without specific revelation. She just went down like a sack of potatoes, clumping onto the floor (fortunately carpeted). She told me later that, during the time she was *out in the Spirit*, she saw butterflies (not stars!). Some consider the life-cycle of these tiny creatures to be symbolic of Christ's earthly ministry – the end or *death* of the caterpillar as Christ's crucifixion, followed by a period *buried* in the cocoon as was Christ buried in the tomb, to finally emerge as a butterfly as was Christ resurrected to new life.

Except for a slight improvement during the 2012 Olympics, when I probably went into *me winning gold medals* fantasies, my mental health continued to spiral downwards. I was like a zombie at Rach and Kam's wedding at the beginning of August 2013 some twelve months later but still managed to give an excellent speech (the 'humility gene' was still not fully kicking in). Things became even worse when, for the first time in my life, I turned to drink. I started buying bottles of whiskey and became very angry when Audrie emptied one of them into the sink. She, very understandably, told me that if I persisted with this behaviour, our marriage was over; and, due to this threat and God's help, the drinking phase did not last long.

By the beginning of September, however, I was almost incapable of writing interpretative reports. Indeed I became so bad that one of my structural engineer clients, Rob Foxton, actually helped me to write them. Even though he had a vested interest as they all related to his projects, it was still a great gesture. The difficulty (for me) with Rob's work was that he had developed a sort of 'niche' market, whereby a goodly percentage of projects related to historic and often listed buildings. So as I'd never had any interest in structures such as church buildings, they took quite a lot of effort to properly describe. Rob, therefore, did this for me, and I simply wrote the geotechnical stuff. I think we did four interpretative reports like this, two at my place and two at his office in Sevenoaks.

On Tuesday 1st October 2013, I went to Rob's office feeling nauseous. This date represented the 30th Anniversary of when I started the business and was also almost exactly thirty three years (6th October 1980) from when I started working for Parky. I felt very rough and found it difficult to drive home. I learned later that Rob and his staff were very concerned over my condition. This was to be my last day in civil engineering – after a total period of approximately forty years.

At sixty years old, I was still clearly affected by not wanting to be like my father. I think it's a well-known psychological fact that many people who have made real efforts to not end up like one of their parents, have somehow done exactly that. I believe that this was now becoming true for me. However, the thing I most feared was weakness whereas, ironically, I reckon I have been pretty strong. Until comparatively recently, it had never crossed my mind that disliking, fearing, or even hating work wasn't normal, and yet I'd managed to achieve qualifications that allowed me to put 18 letters after my name in a subject in which I'd had, at best, only a passing interest. As mentioned earlier, the thought of having 'fun' while tackling challenging jobs simply did not occur to me, albeit that there had been several buzzes and highlights over the years that bucked the trend (quite often during meetings towards the ends of certain projects).

Professional careers, particularly when they're your own business, need a lot of passion and energy simply to keep going; and, during the thirty years, I'd had to manufacture most of my own, in addition to overcoming (and hiding) my strong fears and intermittent panic attacks. When I dropped out of my civil engineering degree course in May or June 1978 I knew that it would take a 'miracle' for me to get back on it. But, of course, I did get back on and managed to survive another thirty five years in this profession, thereby providing for my family. I think that, with me, it was like "God blessing a bad marriage" – without his great help, and at times I certainly felt like a civil engineering imposter, I reckon 1978 would have been the end of it.

CHAPTER SIX

Suicidal

Why on earth would anybody want to commit suicide? I suppose if their quality of life had become so poor, say if they had ended up as a quadriplegic or were blinded by some accident, then the desire to end it all is very understandable. Other people might be ready to pack it all in if they have been suddenly bereaved or felt that their whole lives had been total failures.

Although I did not have any of these reasons, looking back now, there were clear warnings. I had undoubtedly inherited much of my father's anxiety and negativity about work. To push myself so hard and for so long (with so much sole responsibility) in a harsh business environment, was undoubtedly a risk to my emotional well-being. We have also, as a family, experienced our fair share of tragedy and other horrible events. My coping method, as per Paul Gilbert's comments and my earlier referral to burying negative emotions, had been to largely ignore and deny my pain; block it out, and just keep going. I guess most psychologists would consider this to be an extra risk to my mental health, and the term *emotionally illiterate* has been coined in recent years to describe this type of behaviour.

I certainly never considered that I would have mental health issues, let alone want to take my own life, whereas the possibility of heart attacks or cancer did occasionally cross my mind. This meant that when Kev, Rach and Kam started to tell me that I needed to *work on myself*, I can honestly say I did not know what they were talking about. Add to this, *selective perfectionism* (only two buttons – pretty much absolutely flat out or almost nothing) and a real hatred of letting my clients down, then a strong cocktail of fear and stress seems almost inevitable. Nevertheless, it appeared that as long as I had certain props in place, particularly Audrie and health, I could keep holding it together, as I had done for many years.

However, I lost the health prop, which eventually changed everything. Lower back injuries are often the result of long-term stress, and the ensuing consequences are now history. I was undoubtedly very confused by October 2013, due in no small measure to the prolonged use of the addictive and potentially suicide–triggering combination of Tramadol, Diazepam and Fluoxetine prescription drugs. I simply could not cope any more with the awful feelings of nausea (virtually every day for over two years). I tried *everything* - prayer, CBT, hypnotherapy, fear management and other more general counseling, but none resulted in any real improvement. So I eventually lost hope.

What about God? Was He involved? Most definitely, because He healed my digestive system physiologically in July 2012, and I am sure that some of my ability to persevere with work during long-term health problems was down to Him. However, I reckon from His perspective He was looking at someone who had largely lost contact with Him and was misrepresenting His character by having much pride and disrespecting his own wife. I was also misrepresenting God by being a predominantly *adrenaline-filled* rather than a *Holy Spirit-filled* Christian, as I increasingly attempted to live Christianity as an alpha-male and in a muscular fashion. Furthermore, my denial of pain and worrying circumstances, albeit mainly unconsciously, meant that my understanding of other people's problems was very limited. I mean, hadn't Christ said not to worry? – Well yes, but not by going into denial and looking down at those who were. So I think that unbelievably painful though it was, and occasionally still can be, for my wonderful family and me, God had to let matters play out naturally; in order that the guy who said Christianity was primarily about an ongoing relationship with God actually had an ongoing relationship with God.

All people living on planet Earth are subject to 24-hour days. All days are therefore of equal length, but not all are equally important. Wednesday 2nd October 2013 was one such day for me. It was the first of several days when I could, or probably should, have died. As my mental health had continued to deteriorate, I would find it almost impossibly hard to get up, gradually spending more and more time in bed. During much of this time my thoughts had been extremely dark, and, from about February 2013, I had repeatedly spoken to Audrie about taking my own life.

The pressure on Aud during this approximate eight-month period must have been horrendous, and I know she often came home dreading that she would find a corpse in our bed. However, she realised I was extremely unwell, and managed to maintain heroic strength as she patiently and gently continued to tell me that suicide was not any sort of solution; I would get better in the end. However, I was now so far gone that I even believed taking my life would be no different to what might have been the case in August 2006 had I died naturally from pneumonia.

Early on that Wednesday morning, I decided to end my life by taking pills. When Audrie later went off to Kev's apartment to do her weekly cleaning job, I couldn't look her properly in the eyes as I promised not to do anything stupid. Anyhow, very soon after she left, I reached down under the bed for some Propranolol tablets (Beta-blockers) that I'd stopped taking some months before. These were of the sustained, gradual release category, with a recommended maximum adult dose of

160mg per day. There were thirty five 160mg tablets and I took them all (in two batches) with water – that is thirty five times the recommended maximum daily dose (5,600mg or 5.6g) in about thirty seconds.

I looked at the clock. It was 12.10 pm. I felt very calm and maybe even empowered (I was getting out of it all), and wrote a note to Aud, Kev and Rach saying goodbye, that they were all brilliant, and I was so very proud of them. I then simply lay on the bed waiting for the tablets to kick-in. Nothing much had happened by the time Aud phoned up at about 2 pm, just to check on me. I said that I was ok and I would see her later. However, very soon after putting the phone down, I felt real guilt that the last words I'd spoken on this Earth to my lovely and trusting wife were lies. So I phoned Audrie back and told her what I had done. She told me to phone Dr Stokes at the surgery and, for the first time in my experience, unsurprisingly got put straight through.

Dr Stokes told me to immediately phone for an ambulance. I think it must have arrived at about 3pm and, amazingly, the paramedics asked me quite a lot of questions as they filled out some type of form. The tablets were now definitely kicking in, and I was feeling woozy by the time we set off for Frimley Park Hospital. I remember seeing the entrance to the hospital and then must have passed out. It was approximately 3.40 pm.

I think a word of explanation is needed: I suspect that this might be common to many people who attempt to take their own lives, but it's amazing (when you get back to calmer reflection) how unaware you are of the absolute trauma you're causing to those closest to you. I presume it must be part of the depressive illness.

Audrie arrived at the hospital at about the same time as the ambulance and saw me in a cubicle a few minutes later. I apparently told her how sorry I was for what I had done, but that I simply could not take any more. I was, however, too far gone to remember any of this. Audrie said that I was looking very grey and that the hospital staff were extremely worried. They had been told by the paramedics about the massive amount of Propranolol I had taken and had grave doubts, as I lapsed into total unconsciousness, that I would survive.

As it happened, the hospital was fairly quiet (a rare event for Frimley Park) and I was immediately seen by the emergency *crash team*. They were brilliant; moved me to intensive care and kept me going using CPR, including defibrillation, as my heart-beat regularly dropped to single figures. So low in fact that even the slight lifting of my head during intermittent vomiting was considered to be too great a risk to my heart. Audrie also recalls that I was continually fitting violently from about 4.30pm to at least midnight. Kev, Rach and Den arrived early evening, and, at about 10.30pm, Ian Stackhouse and Lance Redman, leaders at Guildford Baptist Church (Millmead), turned up to pray for the family and me.

Unsurprisingly, the *crash team* also did not know if I would survive and at one point considered putting me into a medically induced coma. Aud told me that everyone was sent home in the early hours of Thursday morning, with the promise of a phone call should my condition deteriorate any further. The hospital also said that the next twelve hours would be absolutely crucial but, from their tone, she felt they considered a full recovery (without a major stroke or similar) to be very unlikely.

The home phone rang at about 7am on Thursday. Apparently this is a fairly normal time for a hospital's early call, so Aud briefly agonised that I had passed away. Anyhow, it was Rob Foxton phoning to see if I would be coming to his office that day.

Amazingly I did survive but for a few days was so confused and *tripping* so badly that Aud initially thought I had suffered permanent brain damage. This might sound incredibly cruel, considering the horrendous time I had put so many people through, but it was such a relief to have some release from the continual nightmare of living and feeling sick. I can at least understand now why some people take recreational drugs, even given the fact that these generally screw you up in the end. My *trips* were bizarre and I could relive them even now if I wanted to (which I most certainly don't).

Due to again developing pneumonia, a not unusual occurrence in these particular set of circumstances, I spent a total of ten days in hospital before returning home. This was after being checked out by one of their consultant psychologists, who said that he was convinced I would not attempt this sort of thing again, although I did not know for sure. Aud, of course, looked after me brilliantly and for the first few weeks, I felt more or less OK. The anxiety and nausea did, however, return with a vengeance and, having now finally been taken off Diazepam and Fluoxetine during my hospitalisation, I felt stressed beyond belief for most of my waking hours - being forced to pace continually to get through each day. It is so hard to describe how bad this feeling was. Before getting mentally ill, I might well have thought (although not said) that people experiencing this type of condition simply needed to toughen up and pull themselves together, but it was nothing like that. The best analogy I can think of is that of trying to hold your breath underwater - you can stay down longer if you keep very relaxed, but you have to come up in the end. However, I could find no way of actually *coming up* – there was no release button and everything just kept on getting worse. Alternatively, it was like *having a broken leg in your brain.*

I had a real epiphany moment in December 2013, which hopefully killed off *Adrenalin Man* for good. It occurred when reading a book called, *The Return of the Prodigal Son* by Henri Nouwen, a Dutch Roman Catholic priest[10]. This publication followed days of this guy simply meditating on a painting of the same name by Rembrandt, exhibited in a museum in St. Petersburg, Russia. The whole book is quite profound, but the single truth that really hit me relates to a section where Nouwen explains that you are not able to properly love people if you are always competing against them. I thought, *Man, I've been doing that for over forty years!* It had been my life; and, seemingly, almost untouched by becoming a Christian. I was often comparing others with my *external unreal me*, which was unrealistically higher than my *internal real me*. It was then only a short step to my looking down at some of the people with whom I came into contact.

By January 2014, I again felt that I couldn't take any more of the horrendous and unrelenting symptoms and, by the end of the month, had made a further three suicide attempts – one of which comprised an aborted drive towards the Severn Bridge to jump off, which, not surprisingly, involved the police. To avoid incarceration in a psychiatric unit, I agreed to voluntary daily attendance at the Ridgewood Psychiatric Hospital in Frimley. This was a horrible building much of which dated back to Victorian times. It has subsequently been demolished, and the unit transferred to Guildford.

I had two separate stints of about a week each and loathed both of them. There were various *Activities* in the unit, one of which was called Pat-the-Dog. A lady brought in a dog once a week, and we were to *pat it* – give me a break! I know that the unit nurses and care assistants were

---

[10] Henri Nouwen, *The Return of the Prodigal Son*. Continuum International Publishing Group Ltd, 1997.

trying their best, but this activity alone could make you feel depressed even if you weren't before.

I now began to experience real guilt over all that I had done, and simply could not accept that someone as cool as *Graham Martin* (I had of course been fooling myself) had behaved in such a manner.

My illness caused many awful and diverse times for the family in the first three months of 2014. Aud's eldest brother, Steve, was going through a major heart operation at about this time and she visited him in hospital at Plymouth, leaving Kev and Rach to *dad-sit* as I wasn't well enough to be left on my own. Not surprisingly, Aud was now getting thoroughly mentally and physically clapped out, and it was only her anxiety of what I might do to myself that prevented her from leaving me (for at least a few days) on several occasions. Although very ill, I was still well enough to know that I was putting immense pressure on Audrie, and it was very upsetting when I occasionally heard her telling people things like, "I just don't think I can look after Graham much longer." I desperately wanted to be a man again, but simply could not do it.

One more *factoid* to complete the picture. From January until July, when not in hospital, I received daily visits from the local Home Treatment Team, whose primary function is to support individuals experiencing mental health crises so that admissions into psychiatric units can be avoided or minimised. Although this was an overall positive experience, it did serve to continually remind me that I was very unwell. Indeed my stress levels increased during most of this time as evidenced by a now continuous and more structured pacing on mats with square patterns: two steps forward and one step sideways or one step forward and two steps sideways, as per the knight on a chessboard – and all day!. Life was unbelievably awful, with the possibility of living for, say, a further twelve months not only being unthinkable but completely off the scale.

Audrie went to visit Steve again at the beginning of April, this time at home in Torquay. I was in a dreadful state and believed that I would never again sleep in the same bed as my wife. Before Aud left on the Monday morning (7th), she gave me quite a few *Words* that she had received (for me) from the Lord, as He repeatedly woke her up in the middle of the night. She must have had perhaps thirty or forty of these over the years, and absolutely all of them have been accurately fulfilled; some almost immediately and others over time. Probably representing around half of those given that night, I have selected the following:

> *You have had a false humility* (you can't fool God).

> *Humble yourself under God's mighty hand, and He will lift you up* (in His time, not mine).

> *I have not caused you this pain; I have been by your side.*

> *He's taking down the old, and re-building the new.*

Kev was also right on it when I again started talking about taking my own life:

"Don't argue with God, dad, you won't win."

Kev and Rach again stepped in with heroic efforts, sharing the *dad-sitting* duties. However, Rach, who was staying at our house on the evening of Wednesday 9th, had to get up and leave at about 5am on Thursday for a work shift starting at 6am in Walton- on-Thames. I was left on my own in bed feeling awful, with the medication until the end of the month (a substantial amount, contained in a *Dosette* box) on top of the bedside cabinet next to me. My Community Psychiatric Nurse (CPN), Sian, was due to call later in the day, and then Kev was going to be taking me to Guildford to meet up with Mary Clarke and Ruth Salisbury, a couple of wonderful and very switched on Christian counsellors from Millmead.

I couldn't face any of it so, at about 5.30am, went outside to stick a note on the door telling Sian that I was staying at Rach's and therefore not in - all lies of course, but I was in such a mess. Anyhow, I reckoned that it looked believable as Rachel had borrowed our car for work. I then went back to bed after taking all the tablets - bliss! - yeah right! I did vaguely hear the doorbell being repeatedly rung at some stage (probably Sian), but couldn't have cared less. She must have then gone away, presumably believing my message.

I must digress slightly here to pay tribute to Sian who gave me (and Aud) massive support over four years up to the end of September 2017; going beyond the call of duty time and time again. One of her fundamental work principles was to ensure that very ill people such as I was only attempt tasks likely to result in success, as failure would probably lead to disproportionate, negative effects. This was particularly tested one day when I needed to urgently fill out a (final) VAT form relating to my former business. This was way beyond me and hardly likely to form an integral part of being a CPN. Anyhow, Sian went for it, reading through the notes, and then encouraging and, most importantly, organising me so that I knew which of the basic arithmetic tasks I needed to carry out. And we did it; a success!

On that Thursday (10th), probably due to exhaustive stress caused simply by coping with the situation, Kev had seriously considered not coming to take me to Guildford but then intuitively felt that he had to make the effort. He probably arrived at about 1.30pm - some eight hours after I had taken the pills. I had left the keys in the door lock so that it couldn't be opened from the outside, which meant that he had to climb over the side gate into the back garden. Once there, he could see that I had collapsed unconscious downstairs having collected together lots of family photographs. Goodness knows what was going on inside my head. I have no memory. After kicking in our large French window, Kev rescued me and got me off to Frimley Park Hospital again. So he undoubtedly saved my life or, at the very least, prevented a major stroke.

I woke up in hospital at about 11pm to find Kev and Aud sitting next to the bed. She had been greeted with the news of my latest suicide attempt immediately upon arriving back from Torquay on the train. She is a very strong woman and had apparently managed to take it all more or less in her stride. Anyway, I think they both went home at about midnight, and I was left in the all-night care of a truly awful older nurse – a right old *bag* – and I say that with Christian love!

The following morning I got it into my head that my family had finally forsaken me, hardly surprising given the circumstances, so I just pulled out the various drip-feeds attached to my body. I then quickly and quietly got dressed and walked out of the hospital trying to look as normal as possible. No-one stopped me, and I did not even consider that the police might get involved - I simply had to find my family. I presumed that they would all be at our home or Kev's flat in Sunningdale. Amazingly, I bumped into someone I knew in Frimley High Street, and he gave me a lift home. He and his family were going on holiday to Cornwall, whilst I should not even be at large - it was so surreal. No-one was in when I arrived at the house and I managed to climb the gate into the back garden where, of course, I noticed the temporary timber boarding put up to cover the smashed French window.

I did not know what to do. My brain was in total melt-down. Having climbed back over the gate, I repeatedly walked up and down a short section of the nearby Basingstoke Canal footpath, before finally going for a pint and steak and chips in The Swan pub. When I came out, the family, plus various friends and the police, were all outside our house. One of the neighbours spotted me - goodness knows what they thought. Realising that the game was up, I walked over and handed myself in. I was amazed that everybody was so relieved; evidence, I guess, of the melt-down causing my mind to become so unaware and blinkered.

Having been taken back to Frimley Park Hospital by the police, I was soon transferred to and safely locked up in the Wingate Ward of Ridgewood Psychiatric Hospital. Even the admission process that evening of Friday 11th April 2014 was dire. Audrie thought that the male administrator responsible was actually one of the patients who had been given special tasks due to good behavior. I felt terrible after my family had left, and it was a horrible experience being locked up for the first time in my life, separated from the outside world by two *Fort Knox* doors.

Audrie returned home to an empty house except for our cats, Arnie and Poppy. Animals may not be able to speak but they certainly know stuff and can be very sensitive to our feelings and moods. That first night of separation they slept under the duvet on my side of the bed, right next to Aud – something they had never done before.

CHAPTER SEVEN

The Psychiatric Hospital

Why is light given to those in misery, and life to the bitter of soul, to those who long for death that does not come, who search for it more than for hidden treasure. (Job 3:20-21)

So what to say about my time *in The Unit*? First of all, I am just so thankful that Audrie, Kev and Rach, and the rest of the family, together with our friends from so many different walks of life, really hung in and stayed close to me. I have no idea what would have happened had everyone not been so supportive. I know I had many more visitors than anyone else. The staff were also really good, not that I could pick this up for many weeks. The fact that most of the nurses and care assistants were from Zimbabwe and Nigeria and were Christian, was a massive positive.

I am not, of course, talking here about some sort of cosy little *Christian Club*, but rather that they shone some light into the prevailing darkness of that psychiatric unit. The second thing is that this was a place where I really got educated. I think it is an oft-repeated mistake for those of us who come from a primarily academic background to think that this is the only *proper* education, but it is not. It is only a fairly common and acceptable strand. I spent a total of forty years in civil engineering and twelve weeks in the unit - it is hard to say where I learnt the most.

It was unbelievably awful to wake up on the morning of Saturday 12th April 2014, in a dormitory with three other guys. It was a real shock and for weeks my first thoughts upon waking all related to overwhelming disappointment, sometimes with tears, that I had not died in the night. I had no idea that such desperately low levels of depression could even exist, and discovered that I could not find a single positive thought in my brain. All thoughts were, therefore, my *enemies*; the only, and very inadequate, defense being to count the hours until bedtime when, upon queuing up with the other *inmates*, I could have more pills and sleep, leading to at least some temporary respite from this horrendous world.

This did not mean that I believed the gospel of Jesus Christ to be untrue, but rather that I could not see how it might benefit me at the time (unless I died). My faith in God, as I continued my earthly journey, was completely shot. I absolutely dreaded the wake-up call at 8am by (generally) Asian ladies - "Harro, wake up, bleckfast", but usually managed to stagger down to the canteen for porridge (except Sundays, when there was only cereal - never found out why?). I remember deciding, on this first Saturday morning as I stood in line waiting with my tray that I would never speak to any of my fellow inmates, all of whom looked pretty weird and troubled. I was, of course, completely unaware of how weird and troubled I looked.

Before talking about my own experiences in the ward, it seems appropriate to briefly describe some of the other long and shorter-term inmates:

Roger - A lovely, middle-aged guy who appeared to have been suffering from acute trauma for many years following, possibly, a severe motoring accident involving fire (as he kept talking about *The Fire*). He was very much *in and out*; sometimes being capable of basic conversation and at

95

other times running along the corridors with no clothing over the lower parts of his body.

I particularly remember a very sweet incident one evening, when Audrie was praying for me in the canteen before she went home. When she finished, we looked around and Roger was silently kneeling with his hands clasped tightly together. I believe God loves that kind of simple and very honest prayer. Anyway, it seems that he did honour Roger's prayer because I met him in North Camp, Farnborough a couple of years later. He was the best I had ever seen him, and he told me that he was doing well and staying in local independent-living accommodation.

Kathleen - A D-Day-baby - she celebrated her 70th birthday on 6th June 2014. Normally very placid and lovely, she usually kicked off at about 10pm, shouting the worst possible obscenities at the top of her voice. I have to say that I've never heard language as bad as that, even from the many construction workers I have encountered on site – including 'Davie Hiller the driller', who used the *F-word* so many times that people often had to ask him to throw in a noun or two so they could work out what he was talking about.

Elizabeth – A pleasant lady, probably in her early to mid-forties. She was suffering from some form of Schizophrenia which seemed to have a natural origin rather than drug-induced. She had lots of problems; one of which was that, following her latest attack, her husband had finally given up on their marriage, and they were now going through the painful process of divorce.

Probity – No idea of his original name, Probity was in his early fifties and one of the guys who shared the first dormitory I was in. Although I got on with him pretty well, he was, and remains, the darkest person I have ever met. He had tried to commit suicide on several occasions and, trusted with a weekend away from the unit, did indeed kill himself, leaving an embroidered cross on the bed directly opposite my own. His death shocked me more than I previously would have expected - perhaps a bit of reality was finally beginning to kick in. I couldn't decide whether to stay put, where the related *darkness* was almost palpable or to take up the immediate offer of a move to another dormitory.

Anyhow, Aud's brother, Den, very kindly came to the dormitory and prayed against anything ungodly or evil - the atmosphere lifted quite a bit after this and I felt it was completely OK to stay.

Neville - In his mid-thirties and a friendly (if a bit weird) type of guy. I think that even Kev, as kick-boxer and stunt performer extraordinaire, was rather wary of Neville perhaps believing he was a good fit for a serial killer. He seemed to be the most intelligent of all the inmates, and I talked to him quite a lot, because you could not have anything like an average conversation with most, and sometimes all, of the others. Neville carefully explained to me that he was completely normal, and hadn't done anything meriting his enforced stay in a psychiatric hospital. Oh yeah, apart from setting fire to some business premises after a row with the owner.

Alan – Thirty three years old, and, like several of the younger *clientele*, had ended up in the unit because of recreational drug abuse. His mood could change quite dramatically, although he looked too thin to do any real damage.

Bradley/Brad – Same age as Alan, and seemingly incarcerated for the same reason. Very softly spoken with a lisp, his low self-esteem was obvious.

Julian – Similar age and circumstances to Alan and Brad, except this guy undoubtedly had more severe problems. He used to crouch, often for considerable periods, behind toilet doors, *'hiding from No.4'*. He also had problems with duvet covers when at large, buying maybe five or six and then throwing them all away and then buying some more!

Dominic – A nice guy, although sometimes seemed rather confused (assuming my opinion at the time was a reliable guide). Again of similar age and circumstances to the three above, he was a practicing Zen Buddhist.

Stewart – A very tall and dour Scotsman in his mid-forties. This guy had spent sixteen years in the Royal Marine Commandos, including two 18-month tours in Afghanistan. He was, for a while, in the same dormitory as me. I think he was incarcerated for street fights, during some sort of drink and drug-induced psychotic experiences. Although fairly placid when in the unit, you certainly wouldn't want to mess with him.

Simon –Probably in his mid-thirties, and slept in the bed opposite to me for several weeks. He hardly ever got up, having his medication always brought to him in bed; and one night, during a drowsy sleep, kept mumbling that he was going to kill me. The next day, however, he explained that his murmurings were simply due to the heavy medication he was on – so that's alright then! Simon's situation frightened me, as it looked as if he had now become incapable of any sort of real life – was he simply going to sleep in a psychiatric unit until he died?

Miriam – A very confused lady; again in her thirties. Her husband brought her into the unit amidst loud protests that she did not need to be there. She kept talking about leading worship in a particular church, and went on and on about how we must all "sing a song to Jesus." At first, I felt rather embarrassed, until I realised that no-one, including members of staff, seemed to be at all bothered. I suppose in the grand scheme of all the weird and wacky things that went on in the unit, her outbursts were no big deal.

Jaquelin – I felt sorry for Jaquelin. A middle-aged lady, who also thought there was nothing wrong with her and that she did not belong in a psychiatric unit. She often went on about how this had only happened because she'd taken a single day off work. Sometimes she wasn't around, and I think the hospital gave her little trials to see if she really could cope on her own. However, she always came back and undoubtedly was not *right*. One day, when Aud, Den and me were outside in the secured garden, she just picked up a large stone and, before anyone could stop her, completely smashed in a bay window. She then threw the stone on the ground, and went away rubbing her hands saying, "That feels so much better!"

On the first Monday morning, I was woken up at about 7.45 (that's 15 minutes before *Harro, wake up, bleckfast*) by contractors' vans being parked outside my locked ground-floor window (having your own window was a bit of a perk). Maintenance works were being carried out on the hospital and it was weird, and very upsetting seeing *free* site workers with their door keys, walking along the corridors. This was because I'd supervised quite a few ground investigations in hospitals and nursing homes etc. My first thought was that I should be giving the instructions - "I want trial pits here and here, and an 8m borehole over there". But, unbelievably, I was a patient. I think that is probably the most painful surreal experience that I have ever been through. At one point I said to the foreman that I'd been a chartered civil engineer for twenty five years - "Yeah, right," he facetiously replied although in fairness, he did later seem to believe me. I presume I must have said something *geotechnical*.

The following day I was taken by minibus, along with some of my fellow inmates, on a staff -supervised trip to the nearby Lightwater Country Farm, a fairly popular location for families with young kids. I felt unbelievably awful, a foreigner and observer of the human race, to which I no longer belonged.

As per my earlier temporary stays, the staff did try hard to help us and arranged various activities for the five working days of the week. In addition to the thrilling *Pat the dog*, these included:

- Painting by numbers – not really my thing

- Model plane construction – absolutely useless as I couldn't read the very small instructions

- Coping skills (meditation and breathing techniques) - did not like this, ended up navel-gazing and making myself feel even worse

- Music therapy which consisted solely of hitting various percussive instruments very hard - so incredibly depressing

- Weight-training/Fitness classes - only made me feel ill

- Going for a staff supervised walk - rarely had the inclination or energy to take part

- Various meetings/discussion groups that were sometimes ruined by Miriam and Jaquelin butting in incessantly and talking over everyone else.

So not exactly a positive mentality! However, there was one activity, table tennis, which clearly bucked the trend. Having competed at a fairly good level in my teens, I found I could beat everyone; and this did not even change when players seemingly superior to me turned up at the unit. I simply played above myself, it was weird. Even at my best, I'd never had much of a backhand smash, but I had one in the unit – and it could deal with all sorts of spin – spooky. In any event, I remained the unbeaten champion over the full twelve weeks which may well have been very important to me – even more than normal - and, who knows, may have kept a little candle of hope flickering.

Despite the table tennis, however, I still continued to gradually become more and more depressed, if that were possible. Both Sian and my close family and friends had warned me to stay out of a psychiatric hospital at all costs, and I know that some people have been so broken in units such as these that they left in a worse condition than when they came in.

Certainly, during those first few weeks, I could see no way that I would ever get out, and I know that everyone close to me tried so hard to provide meaningful help. This must have been so very difficult and heartbreaking, as I was such an abject picture of hopelessness and despair. I found out later that all my family regularly scanned my countenance during visits to see if they could spot any little glimmers of hope. I was also particularly upset one day by a very unwelcome, although true, comment by Dr Ali Shah, the *big cheese* and resident unit psychiatrist. He said that Kev was now the *dad* and I was now the *son*.

Almost inevitably, the incredible toll on Audrie was getting worse. Although so strong, positive and loving to me while in the unit, she often used to stop in a particular lay-by on the way home, and just cry and cry. Kev, Rach and Den also visited me many times, and I especially remember one evening when Aud was ill that Kev, although feeling very rough himself, came instead so that I wouldn't be even more upset and lonely.

Perhaps not surprisingly, given all of the above and my immediate past, I tried another four times to take my own life - now a total of nine attempts of varying severity. This was difficult in Wingate Ward, as it was purpose-built to prevent these types of incidents. I consequently never got very far, although one attempt did show that, despite everything, God was undoubtedly still on my case.

The twelve weeks in Ridgewood Psychiatric Hospital comprised a total of seventy seven nights, as I was permitted overnight home visits towards the end to hopefully enable me to acclimatise to *normal* life upon release. Anyhow, as is usual in secure psychiatric units, all inmates, when allowed out under either staff or family supervision, had to hand in any accumulated plastic shopping bags upon their return, as these were undoubtedly health risks for disturbed minds. One time, and one time only, I managed to smuggle in a plastic bag; however, this was the only occasion out of my entire confinement that any search for this item was ever made. The bag was subsequently found and taken off me. Whether I would have been successful (if that's the right word) in taking my own life by this method is another question but, in any event, it was clear that God stopped me from ever finding out.

IN THE UNIT

It is morning in the unit, probably in about the third week of my enforced stay, and I'm sitting in the fairly ghastly communal area. Miriam walks slowly across the large room, handing out two Christian booklets to the others sitting around, who, to my amazement, are really interested and readily take them. I take them as well. They are called "I Am With You" and "For Those Who Are Hurting", and have been written by an Anglican priest, Father John Woolley (1928-2008). They are very good and give me a bit of renewed hope (not easy, when you feel incredibly ill and fighting off severe depression virtually all the time). Anyhow, their distribution by the very confused and unwell Miriam is another example of how God can use those who have real problems as much, or possibly more, than those who have apparently got it all together.

I also received some help from a guy called Brian, who owned a gym in Woking and came in on Tuesday and Thursday mornings to conduct weight-training/fitness classes. Unlike Wingate Ward, which comprised a large single-storey extension perhaps added in the 1960s, the gym was located in the Victorian and major part of the building and had a stale and depressing smell. I had finally begun to take some limited interest in this particular class, possibly because I was stronger and fitter than the other attendees (not that this was saying much though). Anyway, one morning I started to train but was simply too depressed to keep going for long. Brian immediately stopped what he was doing, took me aside, and gave me a very loving and positive talk. I am not sure how much his actual words helped me, but his great concern and effort certainly did. Somewhat encouraged, I began to take *power walks* (well, sort-of) around the garden after breakfast.

Aud, Kev, Rach and Kam had booked a short break in North Devon, taking in the Bank holiday weekend of Saturday 3rd to Monday 5th May. However, probably a day before, both Aud and Kev intuitively felt that this was too long for me to be left alone with no visitors. Indeed Kev believed that God had told him to *prepare for the death of your father* if he went away. So they both decided to stay local - just as well!

Monday 5th May 2014, the 24th day in the psychiatric unit, undoubtedly represents the lowest point of my entire life up to now (and hopefully forever!). I know it also does for Audrie and, possibly, Kev (Rach and Kam weren't given the details until later). My depression and, particularly, the stress symptoms were worsening by the minute and by mid-morning, I was pleading with the staff for even a small dose of Diazepam or any other benzodiazepine. However, Dr Shah was on holiday, and none of the nurses or support-workers were authorised to prescribe drugs like these (they would presumably have been sacked if they did). The World Championship Snooker final was on the TV, and I had to be rooted to my seat in the depressing communal area to hold off Miriam's and other women inmates' attempts to change the channel. By early afternoon I was almost climbing the walls and felt that I would soon have to start shrieking out uncontrollably (as quite a few did). However, I knew that this would do no good – apart from endeavouring to calm me down, the staff were powerless. I've heard of some heroin addicts, in attempts to withdraw from this drug, actually throwing themselves at barbed-wire fences, hoping that the pain would temporarily distract their minds and give them a few moments respite from the continuous agony– that's exactly how I felt. I was definitely into *having a broken leg in my brain* territory. I couldn't take any more and simply had to get out of a body that was experiencing such unbelievable torture.

As Aud and Kev had not gone to North Devon with Rach and Kam, Audrie came to pick me up around 3.30pm for an afternoon and early evening visit to Kev's place in Sunningdale. On the way, she parked the car in the Waitrose car park, immediately adjacent to Sunningdale railway station and the level crossing straddling the A30. I was in a desperate state as we entered the store, and felt that I couldn't face any more; particularly the thought of going back to the unit. Anyhow, as I was looking at the yogurt section in Waitrose, I suddenly realised that this was my opportunity; I was at least fifteen yards closer to the open exit than Aud. I must have deliberated for a few seconds, and then suddenly took off making for the railway and, specifically, *the live rails*.

I knew I had to get beyond their protective boxing-in adjacent to the station and level crossing, and probably ran about thirty yards up the track to make sure. What I hadn't anticipated, again completely blinded to everything except the overpowering desire to end my life, was that Audrie would be sprinting up behind me desperately shrieking in an awful 'unhuman-like' manner for help. There were several people around and although I'm sure they were all very concerned, nobody was going to take the risk of also being electrocuted or mowed-down by a train. I got to the exposed electric rail (750 volts, with a high current) and held my right foot over it for perhaps 2 seconds. It was the most intense 2 seconds of my entire life! I then placed this foot onto the electric rail, with my left foot remaining on the ground – nothing happened! I tried again, this time running over to and placing my foot on the electric rail serving the other line – identical result. What the heck was going on?

Audrie had now caught up with me and was obviously in quite a state. We made our way back to the level crossing, and then some big guy, upon seeing Aud's plight, grabbed me and held me in a vice-like grip until the police arrived. It turned out that an off-duty Network Rail employee *just happened* to be walking across the level crossing at the same time as I appeared running, with Aud close behind and shrieking. Not only did he know how to turn off the electricity supply trackside, he was also close enough to get to the relevant switch in the ten seconds or so that it took me to run up the track and put my foot on the rail. Quite possibly, my delay of about two seconds was crucial in enabling him to do this. Without this, both of us (as Aud may well have been electrocuted herself, trying to pull me off the live rail) would have been killed or severely incapacitated.

Kev turned up shortly before the police arrived, and found out about the guy, a middle-aged man with glasses, switching off the electricity supply. Aud told me later that she thanked him as she was leaving. He simply nodded and smiled; all in a day's work I suppose - although, of course, he wasn't actually at work.

Soon after arrival, the police bundled me inside their car. They were very nice to me and tried to be encouraging during the journey back to Ridgewood Psychiatric Hospital. I hadn't heard about the Network Rail employee's vital contribution to saving both my own and Audrie's lives, so they told me when I asked them why I hadn't been electrocuted and killed. This knowledge made me feel a little bit better because I had hitherto been thinking that there must have been an automatic *trip-switch* or something; and how could I have been so stupid not to have thought of that and made such an idiot of myself. This news then made me realise that God had yet again come to our aid big-time.

In actuality, this was such a big *miracle* that I found myself beginning to doubt it several months later. Maybe the power hadn't been on after all, or perhaps my rubber soles (though well worn) had prevented electrocution. So I found a Network Rail Safety Web-site and, incredibly, this was the first thing I read: *The power is on all the time, even Christmas Day. The survey also reveals that two-thirds of parents haven't discussed railway safety with their children. Furthermore, a quarter of mums and dads believe myths such as being protected from electric current by rubber-soled shoes or that you wouldn't be hurt if you only touched power lines for less than two seconds.*

This is, therefore, further confirmation that only God could have produced such an amazing deliverance from death. Indeed, my good friend Barrie Stevens subsequently had a very relevant Word when praying for me – *I made dead that which was alive* (the electric third rails), *and that which was dead* (me wanting to kill myself etc.) *alive".* Barrie was himself rather taken aback by this, as he had not been expecting any such revelation. And then I even went back to the particular section of railway line (not on to the track of course) to check that, yes, there were sometimes sparks when a train's electrodes contacted the live rails; and thus electricity was indeed present - I mean, how much evidence could anyone possibly want?

This then was the tenth and most serious attempt to take my own life. It was also the last. I was now terrified of ever doing this again. What was God protecting me from if I did kill myself by this method? And what might be the extreme resultant physical and mental health effects if I lived? Kev's *word* to me: *Don't argue with God, Dad, you won't win*, had also been proved true. How could one tiny human being compete against an all-powerful creator God? Yet I was still unbelievably stressed and depressed – in some ways, more so. I had all sorts of wild thoughts going through my head, such as: This is not me. This is not my life. This should not happen to me; it's not what I'm about. This is not what I do. How could I ever have done this? Why wasn't it someone else? I wish I could be anyone except me, even if that means sleeping on the streets. Why can't my spirit take over someone else's less traumatised life, or even live in one of our cats? I even temporarily tried the technique, again inevitably bound to fail; continually forcing myself to pretend that it was twelve months previous and none of these horrendous suicide attempts had taken place.

Audrie was incredibly upset and angry, and the next day (Tuesday 6th May) sent me a text saying, "Now you have actually broken my heart." We are all familiar with the phrase: *Don't bite off more than you can chew*; well, this was exactly how I felt about my life. It was all too much for *little Graham Martin*. I could not cope with living but also, for the first time since I had been so unwell, now really understood that taking my life was no option at all. In the normal run of things, this enlightenment would have led to an even greater, and unimaginable, depth of despair; an experience that was mercifully prevented by the aforementioned realisation that God, by His latest miraculous intervention, was still involved and, ultimately, might indeed turn everything around. This insight also enabled me to eventually come to terms with all the heartache and mental damage I had inflicted upon those closest to me; something that, from a solely human perspective, was probably impossible.

It can, of course, be very hard to find out that the ones you love are not what you thought they were but, from my own experience, I think it is even harder to discover this to be true of your own self. It had turned out that I was not, after all, the hard outer protective skin which had generally served as my identity for over forty years. Richard Rohr is very helpful here, describing how these types of experience can facilitate the "losing of the false self". He then goes on to describe this false self as the role, title, and personal image that is largely the creation of the individual mind and attachments. He also says that it will and must die;

something which often requires an event or set of circumstances too demanding for a person's particular skill set, acquired knowledge, and strong willpower to deal with – so pretty much *spot-on* in my case. He likens the loss of the false self to Christ talking about a person losing their life for His sake and says this loss will correlate directly with how much that individual wants to find their real true self. Finally, he challenges, *How much false self are you willing to shed to find your True Self.* [11] There is a brilliant illustration of this concerning a boy named Eustace in the children's book, *The Voyage of the Dawntreader* by C.S. Lewis[12], novelist and literary intellectual.

On the Wednesday (7th May) when he returned from holiday, Dr Shah prescribed me Clonazepam® (also from the Benzodiazepine family, and again addictive), which gave some benefit, albeit to a fairly limited extent. I was also given a room to myself, a real improvement to dormitory life, and assigned a care assistant as a constant guard. This *suicide-watch* and just being in the psychiatric unit etc. must have been extremely costly to the NHS; perhaps after having paid so much tax during my working life, I was now getting some of this back. Hardly a consolation though, and I remained incredibly depressed and stressed-out. Amazingly, Aud managed to forgive me yet again, and came in to see me that evening. She is an unbelievably strong and loving spiritual lady.

Forward now a week to Wednesday 14th May 2014. Although the extra medication had been of some benefit, the severe depression and stress continued. Everyone involved at the unit was very worried, and I knew that a big meeting with all the relevant professionals, staff hierarchy *and* Audrie and Kev had been scheduled for that afternoon. However, even though I was on time, I simply could not find out the location of this meeting; with the care assistants being surprisingly unhelpful when

---

[11] Richard Rohr, *Falling Upward*. John Wiley &Sons, Inc., 2012, p.85.

[12] C.S. Lewis, *The Voyage of the Dawntreader*. HarperCollins Publishers Ltd, 1998.

asked. I later discovered that, not surprisingly, everyone wanted to discuss my health and situation without me being present. I understand that these discussions were very tense and negative, with all the various professionals agreeing that, without Electroconvulsive Therapy (ECT), I would undoubtedly kill myself.

However, this may well have been Aud's finest hour; because she walked out of that meeting believing that God was in absolute control. He would sort it all out in His time, and ECT would cause me even more problems. It was therefore definitely not His solution. Not for the first time, Aud's baptism verses were coming true – God was indeed walking with her through the rivers and the fire.

THE SPIRITUAL REALM

During our time at SHDC, Ricky Brown and me agreed that Tom Moffat must have been off his head to believe in spiritual beings such as Satan (even discounting his horns and pitchfork) and demons. I guess that many people today would again take this view, and might therefore also be sceptical of 'pictures', 'visions', and 'dreams', plus 'Words' (as previously) that are considered to be of supernatural origin. There are several such instances coming up, and, hopefully, the following quotation from C.S. Lewis represents a balanced and credible position on this matter. It's from the introduction to his classic book 'The Screwtape Letters', a fictional writing comprising a series of advisory letters from a senior demon, Screwtape, to a junior demon and nephew, Wormwood: 'There are two equal and opposite errors into which our race can fall about the devils (demons). *One is to disbelieve in their existence. The other is to believe, and to feel an excessive and unhealthy interest in them. They themselves are equally pleased by both errors, and hail a materialist or a magician with the same delight.'*
(C.S. Lewis, *The Screwtape Letters*. HarperCollins Publishers Ltd, 2012, P.ix.)

The fact that ECT was not God's chosen solution seems to have been confirmed by His apparent involvement over the next few days:

- Thursday 15th May. Aud woken up at 6am, with these words penetrating her mind like a thunderbolt, *The only electricity that will go through him will be mine.* God's aversion to ECT was, of course, consistent with His railway line deliverance – just different types of electricity.

- Friday 16th May. Had a *Second Opinion* meeting with an independent psychiatrist, Charles Bennett. I must have looked pretty rough, as he again confirmed that ECT treatment was now the only option. He told me that the decision to go ahead was, of course, down to me as he could not proceed without my authorisation. Later in the day, I had an unscheduled gym session with June, a very helpful support worker who regularly provided extra sessions simply out of the goodness of her heart. Maybe for the first time, I seriously considered the possibility of Audrie leaving me – so every rep on the various machines was now for *my wife and our marriage*. Somehow I would be a man again and give Aud something positive to love.

- Saturday 17th May. A pivotal day for me. Felt depressed in the morning, but fairly OK after lunch. Audrie, Kev and Rach came over in the evening and, all things considered, we had a pretty good time together. When Kev got back to his apartment, he texted me saying, "I smiled all the way home." I texted him back, ending with, "and I really want to live". I then put on a Christian worship CD – not expecting much, because I had been in a really bad place spiritually for probably several years. In fact, during my last visit to

Mary Clarke and Ruth Salisbury (in February), I had felt terribly uncomfortable and actually on the wrong side of a spiritual divide. This now changed, as something like a *dark heavy cloak* was lifted off and I was immersed and *baptised in love*. It was the most wonderful and incredible feeling (possibly even *electric*), as I danced and leapt around the CD player in my room.

You turned my wailing into dancing; you removed my sackcloth (a sign of mourning) *and clothed me with joy.* (Psalm 30:11)

Both of these experiences have *form*. For instance, I have since come across various accounts of people being freed from depression by the removal of *dark heavy cloaks*, and D.L. Moody, a 19th-century equivalent to 20th-century American evangelist, Billy Graham, talks of a baptism of love from God so strong that he even had to ask Him to *stay His hand* – that is to hold off. Imagine being loved so much that you simply could not take any more. I suppose that is hardly surprising if God's infinite and *agape* (unconditional) love is involved. Anyhow, this was the first day that my life began to turn around, and I began to think and live more positively, even commencing the writing of a journal (became *daily* and still continues). However, when you have gone so far in a wrong and awful direction, it is probably going to take considerable time to be completely put right.

- Sunday 18th May. I have a record in my journal of a *vision* Kev had during a meditation at about 7pm. He told me that he saw a large serpent (a symbolism often associated with Satan) vomiting up a big white egg. Gradually this egg began to crack, and a man emerged from within. He was a happy smiling man. This man was me. The snake then slithered away, never to be seen again. Kev also told me that he had felt uneasy, reluctant, and somewhat shell-shocked during this vision, becoming aware that he was being taken out of his comfort zone.

I believe this experience to be from God and thus completely authentic. This is particularly based on Kev's feelings and reactions, which again have form. For example, the OT prophet, Daniel, says the following after receiving a particularly wide-ranging and mind-blowing vision, *I, Daniel, was exhausted and lay ill for several days...I was appalled by the vision; it was beyond understanding.* (Daniel 8:27)

I have shared Kev's vision with several people in whom I have confidence and trust. They have no doubt that it was genuinely from God and believe that the serpent, Satan, had indeed taken hold of my life (*swallowed me*), but that the egg, the white colour of which indicated purity, represented the Lord's protection. The power of God was too great for Satan who was therefore forced to vomit up the egg so that I could escape to freedom. Various others, including a guy called Sean who had previously been heavily into the occult, repeatedly told me to be careful, as they believed Satan wanted *to take me out*. In my opinion, it certainly looks like it.

- Monday 19th May. A junior doctor came into my room fairly early in the morning to take blood samples before I started my ECT treatment. She seemed quite put out when I said that I had decided not to go through with it. After all, two experienced and distinguished psychiatrists, Doctors Ali Shah and Charles Bennett, had decided that this was the best, and indeed, the only realistic way forward. However, I was adamant – no ECT – end of.[13]

- Tuesday 20th May. A bit of an upsetting day as I was told to vacate my room for a new high-priority case. It was, of course, a lot nicer having your own room than sharing with three other, snoring and feet-smelling guys. Although I got Aud to phone up to try to reverse the decision, my *danger category* had been down-graded and there was no alternative. Anyhow, I managed to calm myself down and was OK by the time I'd finished moving my stuff to a new dormitory. So the ability to do this relatively easily was a clear sign of my improving mental health.

As this continued, I began to interact more and more with the other inmates; particularly, Alan, Dominic, and, the new *maximum-danger* guy, Bradley or Brad. I think Brad had tried to take his life by throwing himself out of a fairly high window and had only been saved at the last moment by a couple of people grabbing his legs and hauling him back into the room.

Brad had very little confidence, so I invited him to one of the activities saying that I'd be really happy if he came along. When he replied, "No you won't", I said something like, "Brad, that's up to me, it's not your call to say whether your coming will make me happy or not!" That seemed to get through to him, and he may even have thought it to be mildly funny. Anyhow, he came to the group therapy or whatever it was.

---

[13] *My father had ECT treatment in the 1960s, which I believe actually resulted in a further deterioration of his mental health. Although modern-day techniques are better than the original methods, several recent specialist studies have concluded that ECT is still dangerous, causing lasting brain damage and memory loss for certain patients.*

We got on well after that. He had a very simple Christian faith, and I think I was able to help him a bit by explaining some of the more basic teachings. I remember also seeing him in the garden one evening at about 7.30, wearing his pyjamas. I said, "What's with the PJs, Brad?" He simply looked at me and replied, "Look, mate, when you've been on the streets in the same set of clothes for six months, you can't wait to get into clean and free pyjamas."

I also managed to get him along to the gym, where he seemed to be a bit horrified concerning how hard I was pushing myself. When he came to leave the unit, he hugged me saying, "Friends forever." And then, just as he left the building, and remembering my rather manic gym training schedule, shouted back "And don't forget, you're sixty years old."

I was also beginning to get on well with Alan. Referring back to what I said about education and its diversity, this guy may not have been an academic, but he was certainly well educated in areas where I hadn't even reached the start line. For instance, he'd held down a job at Morrison's for four or five months (during the winter period), while living in the stair-well of their adjacent car park. I mean, how is that even possible?

Alan also received only occasional visits from his family, and had to do virtually everything for himself; such as washing his clothes and attending meetings with the Citizens Advice Bureau (fortunately situated next to the psychiatric hospital) to sort out all his business affairs. One day he received a letter, seemingly mislaid for several weeks in the unit, informing him that he had to attend an important meeting in Guildford that same afternoon. This was so difficult for him at such short notice, but he did manage it. He was very up and down, succeeding in getting over the high-security garden fence one evening (no pun intended), and, following his early recapture, also trying to hang himself from a bedroom wardrobe. I, fortunately, came across him and stopped the attempt. At first, he was angry and accused me of wrecking his life, but later changed his tune and thanked me.

I had quite a few conversations with Alan about the Christian gospel and bought him a Bible when on an Aud-supervised trip to Windsor. He was well chuffed with this, and, within the next day or two, prayed with me as he gave his life to Christ. I know it will be difficult for him to get spiritual support now he is (presumably) out in the big wide world, but I'm sure that God will take care of him.

One of the things that came home to me when talking with Alan is that we don't all start from the same position in life or have identical forms of nurturing – so assessing our apparent status in comparison with others is never justified.

I also had several good-natured chats about Christianity with Dominic, the Zen Buddhist, although I think we both struggled to fully appreciate each other's position.

After continued, gradual improvement, I was finally released from captivity in the Wingate Ward of Ridgewood Psychiatric Hospital on Monday 30th June 2014, having survived the twelve-week ordeal of being imprisoned with some very mentally ill inmates. In fact, for maybe three or four weeks (when Neville was not around), the only people with whom I could have any meaningful discussions were the nurses or care assistants. I survived for, I believe, three main reasons.

Firstly, God undoubtedly sustained and protected me throughout. Secondly, all my family and friends were unbelievably fantastic and, as I said before, I could never have kept going without the huge support I received. Thirdly, I did somehow manage to dig deep within my soul and thus come out stronger than when I went in. Being in the unit and, particularly, the electric railway lines incident also did much to convince me that I had indeed been extremely ill, and enabled me to more or less come to terms with my various actions and ten attempts to commit suicide. Overall, I would summarise this time as the most horrendous and yet, in some ways, the richest experience of my life.

I was accordingly more at peace over this greatly increased amount of suicidal behaviour than I had been at the beginning of the year when I was driving myself mad (always wanting to put the clock back, which completely does your head in). At that time, I simply couldn't accept that someone as *cool* as me had been capable of attempting to take his own life. The process of forgiving myself had therefore started.

Like the football manager after his team's brilliant performance, it feels wrong to single anyone out, but I am, nevertheless, going to briefly mention two people. Audrie, for her incredible love, commitment and resilience; being able to keep everything on track including being solely responsible for moving house in September 2014. Secondly, my great friend and in many ways mentor, Mike *double doctor* Graveney, for his willingness and ability to talk to me during endless telephone discussions, as a friend, doctor and a fellow-Christian. I must also give credit and great thankfulness to the many people, both in this country and overseas, who prayed consistently for our family and me. It may be difficult to sometimes understand why God considers this activity to be so important, but He undoubtedly does. At the end of the day, *it is not our own weak and often variable faith, but rather His unbelievable faithfulness, that is the true bedrock and anchor of our lives.* I proved this during my incarceration. I was much too far gone for my own faith to be of any help at all, and brilliant though they were, my family and friends could not save a sinking ship that actually wanted to sink! Sometimes only God can give hope. Without His intervention, I would still be in the unit.

I finish this chapter with the following quotations:

From the Book of Mencius (Chinese, 300 BC)

> *When Heaven is going to give a great responsibility to someone, it first makes his mind endure suffering. It makes his sinews and bones experience toil, and his body to suffer hunger. It inflicts him with poverty and knocks down everything he tries to build. In this way, Heaven stimulates his mind, stabilises his temper, and develops his weak points.*

From Derek Prince, renowned 20th-century Christian teacher and author:

> *In my experience, I have found that the people who have been the lowest often end up the highest.*[14]

From Ian Stackhouse, church leader and author:

> *In fact, you begin to wonder, in praying a psalm like this (Psalm 30), whether faith can really emerge until you've known the pits.*[15]

I have no idea how these observations may or may not play out in my life, but I do know that, *The Lord is close to the broken-hearted and saves those who are crushed in spirit.* (Psalm 34:18)

---

[14] Derek Prince, *God's Remedy for Rejection.* Whitaker House, 1993, pp.11-12.
[15] Ian Stackhouse, *Praying Psalms.* Wipf and Stock Publishers, 2018, p.31.

CHAPTER EIGHT

Getting Back on Track & Reflections

Although I was now *at large* in society again, there was still a long way to go on my journey back to full health. A week or two after being released, Kev generously paid for Aud and me to have a weekend together at some swanky hotel in the New Forest. While I had been lining up for meals with my fellow inmates in the unit, I had sometimes looked forward to, or perhaps simply hoped for, the time when I could do this with *normal people* (absolutely no offence to the former intended).

Audrie likes her lie-ins on holidays or breaks, so I went down to the first of the hotel breakfasts on my own. I guess, amongst other things, I had become somewhat institutionalised because this was a total culture shock. Why were people looking so happy and joking and laughing over what seemed to me to be complete trivialities? – it was almost as if they had *spare laughter to burn*. I was in a real state, felt completely alienated from those around me, and couldn't eat much before crawling back to our room. I did improve slightly over the remainder of the weekend, but this had been a pretty nasty wakeup call.

Back at home, I again found it extremely hard to get up, and many times, during perhaps the following two years, did not emerge from the bedroom until well into the afternoon or even early evening. I simply cannot describe Audrie's incredible loyalty, patience and longsuffering throughout; it was truly amazing, and vital to my recovery. I just found everything so very difficult to do and on several occasions my daily journal (at least I usually managed to write that) had entries such as, "cut my fingernails." I mean, for the whole day! Not being able to *do life* is an incredibly frightening state in which to live, something that was made particularly depressing and discouraging in my case by the still vivid memories of the very high workload I had coped with during the last thirteen or so years of the business. And this awful mindset was made even worse by having to throw so much of the entire thirty years work into a large *Household Rubbish* skip at the local tip. It was also quite a shock, even though it had never been that big a deal to me, to realise that all my earning power had suddenly evaporated.

So what about God? Could He have done something to cut short all these truly awful times? After all, He had miraculously saved me and Aud from being electrocuted and suffering horrendous injuries, and also come to our aid in many and various ways. I had certainly not given up on Him again doing something spectacular and indeed, almost from the day I injured my back, had repeatedly been asking for His healing power both in the physical realm and, later on, in the area of mental health.

Here's the thing: is God able to create a weight that is too heavy for Him to lift? If not, then He can't do everything; and if He can, then He can't be God. This type of reasoning is well described by C.S. Lewis: *Nonsense remains nonsense even when we talk it about God.*[16]

And the relevance of this type of argument? Well, can God instantly produce character in, and also instantly form intimate relationships with, human beings. The answer must surely be *No*, because this statement represents a total contradiction or nonsense. And it is here that the

---

[16] Philip Zaleski & Carol Zaleski, The Fellowship: *The Literary Lives of the Inklings.* Farrar, Strauss and Giroux, 2016, p. 293.

Western secular view of things seemingly takes a different path to authentic Christian thought. In particular, it appears that today's prevailing atheistic psychology directs most of its attention towards the urgent removal of all suffering together with the elimination, minimisation and management of any associated negative emotions (commonly in conjunction with medication). Now, I'm clearly up for all of this – give me a *fast-fix* every time, whatever the problem. OK, that's my solution, but the thing is I am not God. I am a limited human being created in His (spiritual) image and, much as I might sometimes want to, I can't return the favour by re-creating Him in mine.

God is, of course, invariably looking at the bigger picture and quite commonly uses the stresses and messes in our lives to bring about changes and indeed transformations. So maybe we should not try and clear up too quickly. Nothing is wasted in His economy, including suffering which, contrary to our usual expectations and hopes, may be His most effective tool. This is consistent with Tim Keller's views who states: *Our faith is largely abstract and intellectual and not very heartfelt.*[17] Negative sentiments that along with a sense of detachment (not *being present*) from many features of everyday living, pretty much describe my spiritual condition as it worsened over a fairly lengthy period. So although I am quite sure that God did not want to see me and the family suffer, He simply couldn't get my attention while life was going along more or less OK. As C.S. Lewis famously put it, *God whispers to us in our pleasures, speaks in our conscience, but shouts in our pain.* [18]

Many people have witnessed to the fact that suffering has strengthened and deepened their relationships with God like nothing else can. Furthermore, there are various studies concluding that where

---

[17] Tim Keller, *Walking With God Through Pain & Suffering*. Hodder & Stoughton, 2015, p.228.
[18] C.S. Lewis, *The Problem of Pain*. Harper, 2001, p.91.

depression has not been experienced (perhaps by using denial as I did), people often assume that they have more control over their lives than is actually the case. So depression may well give us a better understanding of our limitations and how much influence (or not) we have over life's many difficulties and problems. When the thought of just getting out of bed feels like the prospect of climbing Mount Everest, you certainly know that you are not master of your own destiny. And linked to all this is the need for patience, something I find so hard. Although I certainly want this attribute, I need to have it now! Finally, this from an American pastor and psychologist, John Ortberg, *For good reasons, God does not always move at our frantic pace. We are too often double expresso followers of a decaf Sovereign.*[19]

Following on from and expanding the above, one of the things I've wrestled with during my ongoing journey back to full health concerns the sovereignty of God and mankind's free will; or, in plain English, *How much is down to God, and how much is down to me?* This is undoubtedly a massive subject and the many associated books could probably fill whole libraries – I'm not kidding. Anyhow, all of this becomes much more relevant and pressing when you are having a really tough time.

So, starting on the H*eavenly side, what evidence has there been of God's involvement and encouragement* since leaving the psychiatric unit at the end of June 2014? In the first place, I know that I have been periodically strengthened by His power within me, and have also experienced His inner comforting (*Don't be anxious, I've got your back*) during the very worst of times. In addition, Mary Clarke gave me two *Words* on separate occasions.

---

[19] John Ortberg, *If You Want To Walk On Water, You've Got To Get Out Of The Boat.* Zondervan Publishing House, 2001, p.176.

- From the OT prophet Jeremiah, *I will build you up again, and you will be rebuilt* (Jeremiah 31:4). And

- God is working his purposes out, so you don't need to strive.

Much to my surprise, I was also given a *Word* on 9th November 2014, far longer than anything else received before or since, but still incredibly concise and of course, full of love. It came out as one continuous strand, apart from the phrase *"and I will do it in my own time"*, which was impressed upon me about ten minutes later.

Do not worry. Do not put pressure on yourself. It is my responsibility to complete the work I have started, and I will do it in my own time. Be confident, my dear child. Go forward with me. Do not worry about results or what people think of you. You are the apple of my eye, and I absolutely adore you. Do not worry about the pills - take just one day at a time. Remember the loaves and the fish. I can use even your very limited efforts and magnify them greatly to achieve the purposes I have in mind. I do not fail. I am the Lord God Almighty. Stop fretting about what you are going through. I discipline those I love, and I will bring you through into a glorious future. That is my responsibility - Do not fret.

This Word is unpacked in chapter 9 to show its consistency with the Bible and how revelations of this nature can guide us on our respective journeys through life.

One of the leaders of a highly-reputed non-denominational Christian Ministry told me that this Word was undoubtedly authentic and had sent shivers down her spine as I'd recited it from memory. She also told me of her initial hesitancy to listen, as she always found it slightly embarrassing when a particular Word did not appear to be genuine. Incidentally, although I would not have chosen the term *adore*, there is no doubt that this is the way God feels about all of us. So even though I may be largely unaware of much of it, God has certainly been and still is, doing stuff.

Concerning life from my perspective on planet Earth, I eventually realised that staying in bed and waiting for divine intervention was hardly likely to cut it, and, bit by bit, began to increasingly get up in the *am-hours*. And I began to read and re-read the above promises to remind myself that God was actually in charge, and there would accordingly be a very positive final outcome. Although my ability to do this has fluctuated, it has certainly helped overall. Spending time meditating on the Bible and praying has, quite frankly, been a bit of a challenge. Despite Mary Clarke's excellent advice concerning *not striving*, the fact that I have been such a competitive and impatient animal for most of my life means that I can easily default into *fast-fix* and negative self-absorption (*Why am I feeling no better, and maybe even worse, after a whole five minutes?*). So I have found waiting for God's timing to be a difficult and frustrating business, with a strong temptation to take on the necessary personal rebuilding work myself. Yet the truth is that my type of rebuilding will only result in a proud and brittle ego, whereas God's results in a humble and quiet strength. Easier said than done though, especially when the nurturing and reliance upon this ego has been a common everyday experience.

Nevertheless, recent hi-tech forays into the 21st century have proved very worthwhile, and I am now receiving daily Bible study helps on my phone from a particular Christian organisation. Only ten minutes of reading and meditating on these at the start of each day, takes my mind off me, something very beneficial and further enhanced by intermittently repeating little bits to myself – as per John Ortberg, *What the mind repeats, it retains"*.[20] Feeding the mind good stuff is, of course, particularly important in overcoming worry which can easily become a negative habit, whereas positive thoughts and dealing with just one day at a time will have the opposite effect.

This next point is both relevant and important. When people are as ill as I was in the period leading up to and including my time in the psychiatric unit, the worst advice that another person can give is to tell them to stop feeling sorry for themselves and simply get over it. This is horrible. Comments of that nature hinder progress rather than provide any kind of benefit. However, as time moved on and things began to improve, I found that the temptation to feel sorry for myself actually increased. This was because I became aware of a weird sort of power with the potential to manipulate certain situations, simply by preying on the fears of those closest to me concerning what extreme behaviour I might resort to if they did not fall into line with my wishes. Quite frankly, this attitude represents the pits and, thankfully, perhaps because I had seen something of its ugly nature in the latter years of my father's life, I very early on made a vow to stay right away from it. I still get the odd temptation to go down this road when I am feeling particularly rough, but usually I manage to remind myself that it leads to a destructive cul-de-sac where no-one wins. So there are undoubtedly occasions when *digging in* and just showing some guts is the right course of action. Anyway, who wants to end up as a *Billy-no-mates*?

I also slowly became aware that some structuring to my life was essential (hardly rocket science), and so, when I felt ready, gradually built in some regular activities. I started weight-training at a local gym where one young guy recently commented that it was good to see me,

---

[20] John Ortberg, *The Life You've Always Wanted*. Zondervan Publishing House, 2002, p.189.

"still smashing it all up" (he's probably got an MA in flattery, but I'll take it all day long), manning the reception desk at Millmead on Tuesday afternoons (ended 2019), and attending a sizeable men's Bible study course, where I was later asked to consider taking on a leadership role (not the right time, but still a great boost to confidence).

Incidentally, despite significant weight-training improvements, I think the fact that I'm no longer *indestructible* is finally beginning to sink in. Audrie, who is an adult, is helping me with this. On top of these encouragements, writing this book has shown me that I still have a brain that works, even though the civil engineering bit appears to have blown up. Finally, I managed to cope with and enjoy a brilliant 40th Wedding Anniversary Celebration on 26th August 2017, with the seventy or so guests including Gibbo, Jacklaus, BC and Audrie's bestest-ever friend, Jan, three of whom had been at our wedding (BC was living in California at that time).

The above *achievements* have certainly helped me to deal with a life over which I now have much less (perceived) control and one that is far less organised and structured than during the *tight ship* days of the business. Although much of that time, particularly the last thirteen years or so, involved coping with very high levels of stress, there was always a sort of resultant *fix* when a specific project was successfully completed. I guess, from about 15 years onwards, I have been a sort of *achievement junky*. Or, to put it another way, although it is probably OK to be achievement-oriented, there will almost certainly be problems when this evolves into achievement-dependent. *Work-highs* are something I still miss, and I know that writing this book has sometimes acted as a compensatory drug. It is not only cigarettes, alcohol etc. that become addictions, any kind of obsessive behaviour is usually a real problem and often very unfair on those closest to us. Indeed, even on ourselves, because all addictions, whatever their cause, pretty much exclude true happiness.

One insight, which has been alluded to before, highlights the importance of relationship, and particularly how actually knowing and personally experiencing the love of God goes way beyond simply knowing certain facts about Him. Factual information is just no substitute especially if it degenerates, as has happened from time to time, into Adrenalin Man simply winning arguments. Christian knowledge, no matter how good, should never be used as a weapon to gain the upper hand in any debate. It is surely wise to recognise that not one of us human beings has the answer to every single question. We inevitably have only a *worm's eye view* of most things, which can easily prevent us from trusting God's *bird's-eye* vision. To experience God's love and compassion is quite simply on a different plane to all attempted human improvements, with genuine encounters resulting in people becoming more loving and compassionate themselves. This quotation from a ninety nine-year-old Billy Graham is therefore particularly relevant: *Go to your knees and pray until you and God have become intimate friends. I cannot describe to you the joy and peace that He gives you as a result of that daily routine that you have in prayer.*[21]

I have no doubts that this quote is the key to living the Christian life as God intends. Christians need to know the loving presence and resources of Christ available within them, which can then be given out to others, rather than relying on their own limited and often inadequate capabilities. Even though *Billy Graham experiences* have been all too rare in my own life, I have had some; such as my previously described *Baptism of Love*.

---

[21] Billy Graham, *99ᵗʰ Birthday: Notable Reflections*. BillyGraham.org, 7ᵗʰ November 2017.

This is one of the more recent encounters. One Sunday afternoon, while on holiday in the Vale of Glamorgan, I drove to a car park on the cliffs overlooking Southerndown Beach, from where I could see across the Bristol Channel to the red cliffs of North Devon. I was reading my Bible and listening to *Sounds of the Seventies* with Johnnie Walker (not the most conventional approach, I suppose), when the presence of God became almost palpable; a feeling so wonderful that you never want it to end. Although of course, it inevitably does. Nevertheless, it still lifted my spirits and encouraged me for a week or two. Imagine what would happen if I could get anywhere close to Billy Graham's daily routine.

To add a bit of balance to the above, it must again be emphasised that factual knowledge certainly has its place and can often be very valuable. Some of the greatest intellects belong to the theological field (quite often linked with science), and as long as their great understanding leads them towards positive enterprises and facilitates the *living out* of their Christian beliefs rather than personal pride, then good on 'em.

Trusting God becomes progressively easier as our experiential knowledge of Him increases. But it can also be easy to ignore or keep Him at some distance. I remember one speaker saying that he lived for a few years in a house located on high ground some four to five miles from Melbourne. When he viewed Melbourne from this vantage point, the entire city appeared to be only about two inches wide and he could put *it in his pocket*. Of course, as he moved closer to the city, it became much bigger, until finally he was surrounded by huge buildings. Maybe some of us keep God at a significant distance so that we can put Him *in our pocke*t and, as above, remain in perceived control of our lives. We are certainly not doing ourselves any favours.

Occasionally people ask me whether I think the pain and suffering of recent years have been worth it. I suppose, at the moment, the answer is that it has been a bitter-sweet experience. Perhaps the first thing to say is that, without it, I doubt I could have been much use to God going forward. My considerable natural pride as a young man had not properly been dealt with by Christian conversion and, even worse, was very gradually built upon by spiritual pride, eventually resulting in the previously noted significant deterioration in my relationship with God. So again, no doubt with reluctance, He had to finally allow me to undergo genuine brokenness and, I guess, get real.

This has also enabled me to know myself much better, as I have begun the sobering task of becoming acquainted with the *internal real* me instead of the *external unreal me*. Part of this has, of course, involved the acknowledgement of the extreme pain that these horrific events have caused to those closest to me. However, there's undoubtedly a limit on how many times you can apologise and ask for and receive forgiveness. It seems that everyone now wishes that I put these times behind me as best I can and move forward with a positive spirit.

In summary, knowing God and knowing ourselves are intrinsically linked, and I have certainly learnt as much about myself as about God during the recent hardships. As William Shakespeare once wrote, *Personal suffering is the key to self-knowledge* (King Lear). I've also noticed that since my negative emotions have been allowed to emerge and I have experienced extreme physical and mental pain, I've begun to have more empathy with the problems of others; surely a good and necessary change. I believe that as long as we are willing, failure, in whatever form, gives us greater compassion for those experiencing struggles and disappointments. Finally, it has been awesome, humbling, and faith-building to witness God's remarkable protection of my life, although I would, of course, have preferred knowledge of this nature to have been gained from rather more positive life situations than attempted suicides. Unsurprisingly, I have no real insight into this sovereign protection, and why this has not been the case for certain others (such as, for example, Probity) but that is His mystery and not mine. I am sure this type of explanation is not normally given to us mere mortals.

Although I have now more or less come to terms with both my actions and the debilitating effects they had on others, the associated levels of pain and hurt were so intense that even after six years back in freedom there remains a temptation to feel failure, guilt or shame (or all three) over something I can still quite easily convince myself just should not have happened. This tendency must be resisted when at all possible, because any acquiescence will inevitably result in fretting, oversensitivity, irritability, defensiveness and even aggressiveness, in turn leading on to deterioration of relationships.

Nobody, particularly me (as self-criticism is probably the most tortuous and corrosive of all), benefits from any of that kind of stuff which, in my case, can also be fuelled by two further specific lines of thought. The first is that my troubles are simply not worthy of all the havoc they caused, especially when compared with horrendous physical and mental torture such as those suffered by wounded soldiers in Afghanistan and Iraq. However, *a breakdown is a breakdown is a breakdown*, and I can do nothing about it – that is apart from beating myself up and feeling even worse.

The second thought concerns the current high level of my mental health-related medication, albeit that I am now beginning to reduce this slightly. This also intermittently worries me, particularly during those periods when I lose sight of God's promises, with resultant feelings of being trapped and wondering how on earth I could have got myself into such a mess - and envying others who can live life *eau naturelle* without even thinking about any need for prescription drugs. Although, as I said above, I needed to be broken, even now it can be pretty hard going and not that much fun and, as a reminder to myself, I must avoid defaulting into competition mode.

Having described some of the things I should be watching out for, how am I getting on? The biggest test surely relates to my relationship with Audrie. When I was in the psychiatric unit, I promised myself that if I ever got out and still had a marriage, I would cherish and treasure Aud to the nth degree. However, what I assumed to be a *no-brainer* has, in actuality, proved to be more difficult than I had thought. Indeed, it now seems that some of the apparent improvements in character during my enforced stay still needed to be hard-wired in – maybe it's easier to be nice when you don't feel so well and the proud ego is at least temporarily redundant.

This proud ego, however, is a very resilient fellow and started to again raise its head as my health improved. First of all, I began to struggle with frustration and anger, due mainly to the fact that, despite all the work I had put into my career, things simply had not turned out in the way I had hoped. Then, in a largely unconscious attempt to make myself feel better and more significant, I again tried to take charge in our marriage and became rather exasperated that I could now no longer use the business to justify my needs taking preference. *It is one of life's ironies that, along with other similar states of mind such as happiness, any striving for significance is likely to have the opposite effect.*

I had been too ill during most of my time in the unit to appreciate the minuscule amount of control I had over my life, including our marriage, but I now wanted this back *big-time*; something that had of course been wrong in the first place. It seems to me that this need to at least partially control others is often the result of fear controlling certain areas of our own lives. Anyhow, at least I am aware of all this now and intend to make every effort to improve.

It's also important to factor into the overall picture the effects of the immense trauma experienced by Aud and me in our different ways. We both understand that I will never fully appreciate the unbelievable pain and anguish experienced by Audrie during my suicide attempts and so many other stressful events, while she will never fully appreciate the absolute torture of some of my symptoms and what it is like to spend twelve weeks locked up in a psychiatric unit with some very disturbed people.

It's pretty obvious that when you have two people coming back from their own versions of hell, life just ain't going to be that easy. Tensions and related stalemates are bound to occur; particularly when Aud is desperate to vent her emotional hurts and injuries but, because of anxiety over how I might react, feels trapped. She knows, as intimated above, that there is still some degree of rawness in my soul, meaning that I can be overly sensitive to certain comments, resulting in annoyance and maybe even outright anger. Then, of course, it is too easy to get into tit-for-tat…and on we go.

So what to do when things are beginning to kick-off? Audrie used to have a fridge magnet which said, *I didn't say it was your fault, I just said I was going to blame you.* And one of Kev's stunt buddies, upon hearing about any distress to his mates caused by, say, relationship breakups has the stock answer – "just go out and buy a new bike!" Anyhow, as the latter option has not been readily available to me, I try to take the lead by sucking it all up. I know I do this very imperfectly and that Aud still has to pick up some of the pieces, but any approach that doesn't focus on humility and the letting go of pride by backing down and admitting personal faults (however foreign and disagreeable this feels) is hardly likely to be successful.

Counterintuitively, this course of action actually represents strength of character, which will only get stronger as the process is repeated. As a friend recently said to me, "The stuff you do (and the way that you do it) does stuff to you" - that is it changes us for better or worse. And improvements in our relationship are bound to occur as the still comparatively recent damaging events recede into the background, and we both become stronger and bigger people.

Finally, it's necessary to point out that there will almost certainly be a spiritual dimension to all of this. Returning to C.S. Lewis and *The Screwtape Letters*, and a particular conversation where Screwtape is advising Wormwood on how to bring about the demise of a certain human being and his marriage. *My dear Wormwood, blah, blah.....When two humans have lived together for many years, it usually happens that each has tones of voice and expressions of face which are almost unendurably irritating to the other. Work on that.*[22]

I am sure that this kind of *attack* has affected both Aud and me, and, at least for my part, confirmed the saying, *old habits die hard*. In addition to this, I have periodically struggled with the fact that certain areas of my soul have been laid open to others, and particularly Audrie, to depths well beyond my preferred and normal comfort zone. I believe we all like to keep certain parts of our minds hidden from even our partners, and can feel exposed, vulnerable and even agitated when these are known about and, wittingly or unwittingly, used against us.

Despite the anticipated future challenges and the fact that I am very much *'a work in progress'*, I feel pretty positive overall. I was going deeper and deeper into the valley of despair during the spring of 2014, but ever since God's baptism of love I have been climbing up one of the sides. I know that what has happened to me is far too serious for it not

---

[22] C.S. Lewis, *The Screwtape Letters*. HarperCollins Publishers Ltd, 2016, p.13.

to have a defining effect, but with the right attitude, this can surely lead to a positive rather than a negative reshaping. Many things in God's kingdom appear to be upside down (actually it's us humans that are the wrong way up), but there is no doubt that He is the *helper of the helpless* and specialises in turning around seemingly hopeless circumstances to give people hope, new starts, and new futures. So having gone from *bitter-bitter* to *bitter-sweet*, bring on the final *sweet-sweet* stage.

Before leaving this subject, it must be emphasised that just because it is possible to learn and move forward from every experience, no matter how bad, it does not mean that everything, past and present, is *all-good*. Some of the things I did were simply wrong, and God, although He knew He could ultimately use them positively, was hardly rubbing His hands with glee. This is deep water, but I am sure that He would much prefer that I had been able to heed, respond, and grow from His previous less severe warnings (particularly as given through Audrie) so that it had not been necessary for me and my family to experience such extreme pain.

Our brilliant 40th Wedding Anniversary Celebration also moved us along a few steps in the right direction, and while we were waiting on a long red carpet to renew our vows it did feel like old times when it was just Aud and Graham; there was still chemistry between us and we were still soul-mates. On a personal note, this was also a real breakthrough for me. I, later on, made a speech of about twelve or thirteen minutes without notes which, trying to be a bit more humble this time, was well received. Having spent such a long period not being able to do things that healthy individuals take for granted, as per my *cut-fingernails-day*, it was encouraging to be able to turn it around a bit and actually do something that many people find difficult and daunting.

So, for various reasons, I was now again becoming a man and husband to Audrie, an improvement that has continued, albeit fairly slowly, over the past three years. This event, therefore, provided a line in the sand, showing me that I was making real progress. Very encouraging, as mental illness, unlike many physical ailments, generally involves significant fluctuations which make it difficult to reliably detect improvement.

Sustained help from family and friends has undoubtedly made a major contribution to my recovery thus far, and I must particularly mention that, back in February 2015, Kev paid for me to have a winter sun break with him in Goa, India. This was very enjoyable and, not surprisingly, another important early step along the road towards total rehabilitation.

I have no idea, as I come to the end of this chapter, whether these reflections appear to be somewhat on the negative side; but this is certainly not my intention, which is simply to describe the most important features of my recent enlightening as best I can without pulling any punches.

In any event, putting these observations down on paper has certainly been very cathartic and instructional. One of the things that this exercise has particularly revealed, is how much progress, spiritually and psychologically, Audrie has made during our marriage compared to me. In the early days, Aud had certain problems arising from her tough upbringing, which, with some help from me, she eventually sorted out and moved on. However, the fact that I generally did not acknowledge emotional problems, but denied and buried them, seems to have prevented similar progress in my case – so I got stuck. Even though I have now 'done a 180', those decades of missed growth will undoubtedly take some catching up.

To finish on a positive note, C.S. Lewis once wrote that, *Joy is the serious business of Heaven,*[23] a core attribute of God that is hopefully evident from these final two quotations:

Firstly, Bear Grylls, the Irish adventurer, writer and television presenter:

To me, my Christian faith is all about being held, comforted, forgiven, strengthened and loved - yet somehow that message gets lost on most of us, and we tend only to remember the religious nutters or the God of endless school assemblies.[24]

Secondly, as attributed to the 1924 Olympic 400m gold medalist, Eric Liddell, in *Chariots of Fire*, the best film ever made:

God made me for a purpose, and that purpose is China. But he also made me fast, and when I run I can feel his pleasure.[25]

[23] C.S. Lewis, *Letters to Malcomb: Chiefly on Prayer*, Geoffrey Bles, 1964, pp.92-93.

[24] Bear Grylls, *Mud, Sweat and Tears,* Channel 4, 2012, p.114.

[25] *Chariots of Fire*, script by Mike Bartlett, Warner Bros, 1981.

CHAPTER NINE

When God Speaks

As previously, the Word I received on 9th November 2014 is as follows:

> *Do not worry. Do not put pressure on yourself. It is my responsibility to complete the work I have started, and I will do it in my own time. Be confident, my dear child. Go forward with me. Do not worry about results or what people think of you. You are the apple of my eye, and I absolutely adore you. Do not worry about the pills - take just one day at a time. Remember the loaves and the fish. I can use even your very limited efforts and magnify them greatly to achieve the purposes I have in mind. I do not fail. I am the Lord God Almighty. Stop fretting about what you are going through. I discipline those I love, and I will bring you through into a glorious future. That is my responsibility - Do not fret.*

Before commencing a piecemeal appraisal of this Word, which came out as one continuous strand apart from the phrase *"and I will do it in my own time"*, impressed upon me about ten minutes later, I need to highlight a couple of important features: Firstly, as might be expected, it is full of love. Secondly and quite incredibly given my tendency to often use more words than necessary, this Word is so unbelievably concise. I simply do not write, talk, or even think in such a way.

Do not worry.

What a great start. Even though God does not want us to worry, He knows that we do, and is happy to come alongside to help. The closely related phrases, *Do not be afraid* and *Fear not,* are used throughout the Bible, numbering sixty nine times in Luke's gospel alone. For instance, *Do not be afraid* immediately precedes the announcement by an angel (probably the archangel Gabriel, so pretty freaky) of Christ's birth to totally terrified shepherds. And there are many other similar meaning phrases. God tells the OT leader, Joshua, *Be strong and courageous. Do not be terrified; do not be discouraged, for the Lord your God will be with you wherever you go.* (Joshua 1:9)

Do not put pressure on yourself.

Again God knows what we are like and that people often put more pressure on themselves than they receive from other sources. It can be quite easy to beat ourselves up over relatively small things.

It is my responsibility to complete the work I have started.

One of the things that I am still trying to fully appreciate myself is that the whole thing is God's show and, unlike us, He always knows exactly what action to take. And He never gives up. This is from the Apostle Paul's letter to the Philippians[26], *...being confident of this, that he who began a good work in you will carry it on to completion until the day of Christ Jesus.* (Philippians' 1:6)

---

[26] The Apostle Paul, whose contributions are referred to regularly in part 2, wrote about 30% of the New Testament, with the *Philippians* being the believers in the newly formed church at Philippi.

...and I will do it in my own time.

I am learning a lot about this from my incredible little grandson, Leon. Everything has to be done *now*! It simply *can't* wait. He, of course, has no idea of the possible reasons, some of which may well relate to grave danger, why certain things cannot be done immediately. And I am like that as well! – on occasions. I believe that if I also continually repeat the word *please* in an ever higher octave, I will get a better hearing. Even though I know that God has a global view whereas I have barely a worm's-eye view, I still regularly think that my understanding of when something should happen is better than God's. But that makes no sense because God always places great importance on bringing certain things to fruition according to His specific and perfect timing. Indeed there are many relevant phrases throughout the Bible such as, *...which God will bring about in his own time...* (1 Timothy 6:15), *But when the set time had fully come, God sent his son* (Jesus).... (Galatians 4:4), *The right time for me* (Jesus) *has not yet come* (John 7:6), *until the times of the Gentiles are fulfilled* (Jesus)... (Luke 21:24b)

Be confident, my dear child. Go forward with me.

Particularly intimate and again emphasising that our life's anchor should be the agape-loving Father God rather than ourselves. These words of Jesus come to mind, *Come to me, all you who are weary and burdened, and I will give you rest. Take my yoke* (see part 2) *upon you and learn from me, for I am gentle and humble in heart, and you will find rest for your souls. For my yoke is easy and my burden is light.* (Matthew 11:28)

Do not worry about results or what people think of you.

This is the bane of many of our lives. We nearly always want to have concrete evidence concerning what's in front of us (not that this is never the correct attitude) and have a great need to be approved of by others.

John's gospel says this about the Jewish religious leaders at the time of Jesus, *for they loved praise from men more than praise from God*. (John 12:43)

It seems to be a general truth that we base our self-image mainly on what we think the most important person (or people) in our life think(s) of us. All well and good if this is God, who is always faithful and trustworthy, but not such a good bet when it comes to other, periodically fickle, human beings. The key potential problem is, therefore, one of too much dependency on other peoples' approval. I'm certainly not saying that we shouldn't give a fig about what others think of us and behave accordingly.

You are the apple of my eye, and I absolutely adore you.

I have already pointed out that I am only saved from embarrassment because I know that God feels this way concerning all of his human creation. In any event, he is here interacting with the previous statement and, by revealing the much superior flip-side of the coin, giving me the platform to seek his approval before looking to others. Jesus said, *As the Father has loved me, so have I loved you.* (John 15:9) This is a truly amazing declaration and our lives would be transformed if we could get hold of even 10% of it.

Do not worry about the pills – take just one day at a time:

Another *Do not worry* statement and again right on the money because, as before, I hate my dependence on prescription drugs (even though it's very slowly decreasing). My take on this is that God has it in hand and I am to simply trust him to sort this out in his own time. As far as the second part of the sentence is concerned, the clear message is to be happy with each day and not be constantly ruminating on possible future outcomes. Jesus says this, *Therefore do not worry about tomorrow, for tomorrow will worry about itself. Each day has enough trouble of its own.* (Matthew 6:34) Notice that Christ is not here saying that we shouldn't plan for the future, but that we need to avoid unnecessary stress and energy-drain concerning matters that can't be dealt with in the short-term – such as my medication.

Remember the loaves and the fish. I can use even your very limited efforts and magnify them greatly to achieve the purposes I have in mind.

This refers to the times when Jesus used tiny amounts of food to feed huge crowds. If we just give Him what we have, He will do the rest. The Apostle Paul says this, *Now to him who is able to do immeasurably more than all we ask or imagine, according to his power that is at work within us...* (Ephesians 3:20) Again, this is pretty incredible stuff.

I do not fail. I am the Lord God Almighty.

In this case, the second short sentence provides the reason for the first. At the start of the Ten Commandments, God tells his ransomed people who He is and what He's done. *I am the Lord your God, who brought you out of Egypt, out of the land of slavery.* (Exodus 20:2) In other words, this revelation gives these individuals some idea of whom they are dealing with and should hopefully enable them to be confident.

It's the same in my case; although given the immense universe with its billions of galaxies and trillions upon trillions of stars, it does seem a bit crazy for the Creator of the whole shebang to be prepared to communicate in this intimate fashion with an ordinary bloke like me. But he is! And, of course, not only with me, but with everyone. As mentioned at the outset, I could never have made up stuff like this, and, particularly, not in this incredibly concise format. Meditating on just these ten words has been a great help.

Stop fretting about what you are going through:

However understandable it may seem, fretting rarely helps. Indeed, it says in the Psalms, *Do not fret – it leads only to evil.* (Psalm 37:8b) This doesn't mean that fretting can always be avoided, because some circumstances are simply too dire. Nevertheless, these few words are still informing us that we should get out of such a mindset as soon as we possibly can; otherwise, we will probably do damage to both ourselves and others. And for me, the most positive thing to do when tempted in this manner is to concentrate on the promise that God Himself is dealing with my problems and, although it may not always feel like it, He is not going to fail.

I discipline those I love.

We see plenty of this in both the Old and the New Testament, with the letter to the Hebrews being right on point. *Our fathers disciplined us for a little while as they thought best; but God disciplines us for our own good, that we may share in his holiness. No discipline seems pleasant at the time, but painful* [no kidding!]. *Later on, however, it produces a harvest of righteousness and peace for those who have been trained by it.* (Hebrews 12:10)

God always reaches out with unconditional love which, however unpleasant it may seem in the short and medium term, regularly includes *tough-love*. Otherwise, similar to children whose parents always give in to their selfish demands, we would all end up as spoilt brats.

And I will bring you through into a glorious future.

Another great promise! The word *glorious* and its derivatives, such as *glory*, are used, most times in connection with God, more than five hundred times in the Bible. It is, therefore, a real *God–word*, with synonyms such as, wonderful, marvellous, magnificent, superb, sublime, etc. (in my opinion) coming up well short. In any event, it speaks of very exciting and fulfilling times. Does it refer to this life or the eternity to come? – I think both.

That is my responsibility – Do not fret.

This is God's brilliant summary and reminder to lean completely on Him and His abilities and faithfulness. As it says in *Proverbs 3, Trust God from the bottom of your heart; don't try to figure out everything on your own. Listen for God's voice in everything you do, everywhere you go; He's the one who will keep you on track.* (Proverbs 3:5-6 MES[27])

The foregoing fifteen connected biblical references, which might in themselves be deemed a reliable spiritual road-map, testify strongly to the authenticity of this Word, God's voice never being at odds with what He says to us through Scripture. I have additionally checked the genuineness of the Word with several mature and experienced Christians whom I trust, and addressed the reliability and trustworthiness of the Bible itself in part 2.

So what is my main reason for writing part 2? The following short 'advertising blurb' hopefully explains. Many years ago, when I was still a student, I went to a meeting where a visiting speaker was questioned over his decision to make the preaching of Christ's gospel a life priority. His answer was very straightforward, "I simply try and get people to take on Jesus Christ". In other words, let's get past those Christians who seem to be weirdos, past what we might perceive to be boring and irrelevant church services, past the rather odd clothing worn by leaders of certain denominations, and go straight to the heart of the matter. In

---

[27] The Message Bible, *Navpress, 2005.*

the end, the only thing that matters is Jesus Christ with his claims to deity and a spotless character, apparently accredited by a physical resurrection after three days. Find any flaws in any of that lot and the whole Christian edifice comes tumbling down. Thus although part 2 covers many different topics, the underlying and principal purpose is to unpack and link these in an interesting and readily understandable format so that, when it comes to the possibility of continued and indeed wonderful existences beyond the grave, informed and meaningful decisions can be made. Is there anything more important than that?

This final thought is from Jim Elliot, 20th-century American missionary:

He is no fool who gives what he cannot keep to gain what he cannot lose.[28]

---

[28] Jim Elliot. *https://www.goodreads.com/quotes/2919-he-is-no-fool-who-gives-what-he-cannot.*

Lightning Source UK Ltd.
Milton Keynes UK
UKHW021823230922
409334UK00010B/1777